Public-Nonprofit Collaboration and Policy in Homeless Services

"*Public-Nonprofit Collaboration and Policy in Homeless Services* offers invaluable insights into the nature and workings of homelessness networks across the United States. The authors' build their chapters from extensive literature sources in several academic disciplines. The chapters on the challenges on collaboratively leading networks, cross-sector medical services, and measuring effectiveness provide particularly important and useful contributions to knowledge for scholars and practitioners."

—J. Steven Ott, *Professor Emeritus, Department of Political Science, University of Utah, Salt Lake City, UT, USA*

"This book provides a novel and timely examination of multi-sector collaboration in addressing the needs of people experiencing homelessness. Both students and practicing professionals will benefit from the authors' critical analysis of relevant theories and practices for designing, governing, and managing collaborative solutions. The book's coverage of health services for homeless populations is an especially valuable resource for the social, medical, and public health fields."

—Glen P. Mays, Ph.D., *Professor, Department of Health Systems, Management and Policy, University of Colorado, Denver, CO, USA*

Hee Soun Jang · Jesús N. Valero

Public-Nonprofit Collaboration and Policy in Homeless Services

Management, Measurement, and Impact

palgrave
macmillan

Hee Soun Jang
Department of Public Administration
University of North Texas
Denton, TX, USA

Jesús N. Valero
Department of Political Science
University of Utah
Salt Lake City, UT, USA

ISBN 978-3-031-11917-0   ISBN 978-3-031-11918-7   (eBook)
https://doi.org/10.1007/978-3-031-11918-7

Cover credit: © Melisa Hasan

This Palgrave Macmillan imprint is published by the registered company Springer Nature
Switzerland AG
The registered company address is: Gewerbestrasse 11, 6330 Cham, Switzerland

PREFACE

Homelessness in America continues to be a challenge facing communities. According to data from the U.S. Department of Housing and Urban Development (HUD), approximately 17 people per 10,000 experience homelessness each day in America and the counts have been growing since 2016. To help people step out of homelessness, we know that the interventions vary from person to person but the program and service needs are common: permanent housing, well-paying jobs, access to health care, transportation support, and more. From a policy and practical perspective, coordination between levels of government and cross-sector agencies is critical in order to build commitment to tackle the incidence of homelessness through pooling community resources together. The Continuum of Care program designed by HUD promotes community-wide commitment to achieve effective coordination among diverse community stakeholders as well as state and local governments. The cross-sector members of Continuum of Care networks work together to address challenges surrounding homelessness and ultimately end homelessness.

Many questions, however, remain unanswered about what these homeless service networks look like, how they are designed, who leads and manages them, and the degree to which they are effective in achieving success. This book makes this direct attempt at answering these critical questions about the Continuum of Care program, a novel mechanism used quite commonly across the United States as the primary U.S.

strategy by which to address the needs of people experiencing home-lessness. While the lessons learned are specifically focused on homeless services, we believe that our findings and theoretical and practical applications are relatable to other complex health and human service policy areas that require and/or demand collaboration of cross-sector actors.

In the chapters that follow, we explore the various elements and complexities of what we call Continuum of Care (CoC) homeless service networks[1]. In Chapter 1, we begin with a background on homeless federal policy in the United States including key definitions of home-lessness, figures and trends on homeless populations, and the various policies at work to address homelessness. In Chapter 2, we dig deeper into what CoC homeless networks look like, with particular attention to their design, member composition, and nonprofit leadership. Chapter 3 builds on the design of networks by discussing the governance arrangement of CoC homeless networks. Chapter 4 discusses the role of individual leadership style and the degree to which it matters in leading networks.

While the work of CoC homeless service networks is varied, we place particular attention to their efforts in the area of health care and assess the degree to which homeless networks make efforts to address the healthcare needs of homeless people and the factors associated with their success in this area (the focus of Chapter 5). In Chapter 6, we present measuring network performance and the multiple ways that managers can assess whether their network is achieving successful outcomes. Finally, we conclude with a review of our key findings, directions for future research, and contributions to theory and practice.

---

[1] In this book, we use the following terms interchangeably: CoC homeless networks and homeless networks.

Acknowledgments

We are grateful to the many that helped make this book a reality.

First and foremost, we are thankful to our students and colleagues from the University of North Texas and University of Utah for their assistance and contribution to our research process. Our journey to study homeless policy and collaboration began in the MPA program at the University of North Texas when a student group prepared a research presentation about the local homeless network in Denton, Texas. That sparked our interest and the start of a passion for understanding the dynamic and challenging processes involved in collaborating to help people step out of homelessness. Special thanks go to Dr. Steve Ott and Dr. Lisa Dicke whose mentorship and never-ending source of encouragement and good advice were invaluable. Dr. Federickia Washington, Dr. Jihoon Jeong, Dr. Kyungwoo Kim, Dr. Younghwan Jeon, and Sara Ford were instrumental at various stages of data collection, writing, and editing of our book.

We are deeply grateful to our dear friend, the late Dr. Kyujin Jung, for his inspiration and passion in research and service. His excitement for pursuing research and generating new knowledge and training the next generation of public administration scholars was infectious and dearly missed.

We have also learned and appreciated the support from inspirational and authentic community leaders working in the frontlines and advocating for people experiencing homelessness, including: Jeremy

Everett (Texas Hunger Initiative), Michelle Flynn (The Road Home, Utah), Mike Nichols (Coalition for the Homeless in Houston), Dr. Adi Gundlapalli, (University of Utah), Dr. David Woody (The Bridge, Homeless Shelter in Dallas), and Gary Henderson (United Way Denton County). We are particularly thankful for your creating opportunities for us to engage with your organizations, for us to tap into your expertise, and offering fresh and innovative ideas for how to think about the importance of collaborating to end homelessness.

We are also in appreciation to the hundreds of homeless network leaders across the country who participated in our research process via interviews and survey completions. Without their input, knowledge, and expertise, our research would simply not be possible.

Much of the work in this book is the product of grant funding support from the Robert Wood Johnson Foundation and the IBM Center for the Business of Government. We are thankful for their generous research funding that made our national study of homeless networks possible. Specifically, the IBM grant funded the national survey focused on leadership in networks, which is the focus of Chapter 3. Data used in Chapter 5 was developed with funding support from the Robert Wood Johnson Foundation.

We would also like to express our gratitude to reviewers of our work and to Palgrave MacMillan for the wonderful opportunity of achieving this book publication and the thorough and seamless guidance through this publication process.

Lastly, we would be remiss without acknowledging our family's support and encouragement. The first author would like to acknowledge her best friend and husband, Dr. Jin Hwan Lee, and her son, Shiwoo. The second author is grateful to his partner Miguel Perez for his never-ending love and support.

CONTENTS

LIST OF FIGURES

LIST OF TABLES

CHAPTER 1

Homeless Policy and Collaboration in America

Abstract This chapter introduces key definitions, factors that are associated with homelessness, and the multilevel policies that shape community programs in order to provide for the Continuum of Care needs of people experiencing homelessness. We offer readers an understanding on the U.S. federal homeless policy, with attention to the HEARTH (Homeless Emergency Assistant and Rapid Transition to Housing) Act of 2009 and more specifically, the Continuum of Care (CoC) program. Communities are expected to design and implement a Continuum of Care (CoC) network as a mechanism to engage cross-sector actors in community-wide planning, pooling resources, and coordinating services for individuals experiencing homelessness. This introductory chapter ultimately provides foundational information from which later chapters of the book build on.

Keywords Homelessness · HEARTH (Homeless Emergency Assistant and Rapid Transition to Housing) Act · Continuum of Care (CoC) Program · Point-in-Time homeless counts · Unsheltered youth

Communities across the United States are grappling with the incidence of people experiencing homelessness. People, regardless of age, race, ethnicity, and background, can and do fall victims to a lack of permanent shelter, and it then becomes the duty of governments and community organizations to find solutions that help people step out of homelessness. These entities must do so following a complex web of resources, stakeholders, and policies that both help and constrain their ability to support the multidimensional needs of homeless people. This first chapter presents an up-to-date analysis of federal homeless policy and offers a comprehensive understanding about the unique local community-focused policy approaches which are carried by cross-sectoral actors.

This chapter begins by unpacking key definitions, factors that are associated with homelessness, and the multilevel policies that shape community programs in order to develop a framework by which to understand U.S. homeless policy and the collaboration that is necessary to provide for the Continuum of Care needs of people experiencing homelessness.

DEFINING HOMELESSNESS

We begin by reviewing key definitions of homelessness as developed by the U.S. Department of Housing and Urban Development (HUD) and the U.S. Department of Education. We also review emerging definitions of homelessness that while not captured in current definitions, are critical to understanding the whole variety of people who experience homelessness.

First, HUD defines homelessness[1] as:

- Individuals and families who lack a fixed, regular, and adequate nighttime residence;
- Individuals and families who will imminently lose their primary nighttime residence;
- Unaccompanied youth and families with children and youth who are defined as homeless under other federal statutes who do not otherwise qualify as homeless under this definition; and
- Individuals and families who are fleeing, or are attempting to flee, domestic violence, dating violence, sexual assault, stalking, or other dangerous or life-threatening conditions that relate to violence against the individual or a family member.

[1] USICH Strategic Plan 2020.

According to the 2020 Annual Homeless Assessment Report, a total of 580,466 people were experiencing homelessness across the United States. Of these, a total of 226,080 were unsheltered. As depicted in Fig. 1.1, the overall counts of homeless people as well as that of unsheltered homeless people have been rising since 2016.

Second, the Department of Education defines homeless youth and children as those who lack a fixed, regular, and adequate nighttime residence. This definition includes children and youth[2]:

- Who are sharing the housing of other persons due to loss of housing, economic hardship, or a similar reason; are living in motels, hotels, trailer parks, or camping groups due to the lack of alternative adequate accommodations; are living in emergency or transitional shelters; or are abandoned in hospitals;
- Who have a primary nighttime residence that is a public or private place not designed for or ordinarily used as a regular sleeping accommodation for human beings;
- Who are living in cars, parks, public spaces, abandoned buildings, substandard housing, bus or train stations, or similar settings; and
- Migratory children who qualify as homeless.

A significant difference between this definition and that adopted by HUD is the inclusion of those who are sharing residence with another person or doubling up with others. According to data gathered from the McKinney-Vento Education for Homeless Children and Youth Program (EHCY), there were a total of 1,508,265 children and youth experiencing homelessness in the 2017–2018 school year—a 122% increase from the 679,724 reported in the 2006–2007 school year.[3]

As noted in Fig. 1.2, the number of unsheltered youth under the age of 18 has been decreasing since 2017. A total of 3,389 unsheltered youth were counted as experiencing homelessness on a single night in January of 2020.

[2] https://youth.gov/youth-topics/runaway-and-homeless-youth/federal-definitions.

[3] https://www.usich.gov/resources/uploads/asset_library/USICH-Expanding-the-Toolbox.pdf.

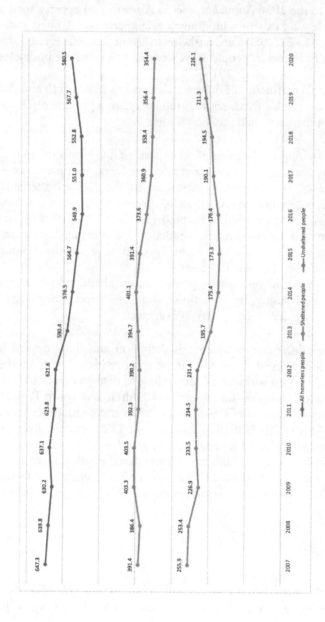

Fig. 1.1 Point-in-time counts of homeless people, 2007–2020 (in thousands) (*Source* HUD Point-in-Time)

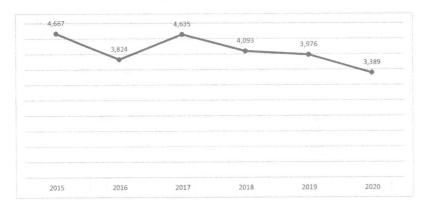

Fig. 1.2 Number of reported unsheltered youth (*Source* HUD Point-in-Time)

FACTORS EXPLAINING HOMELESSNESS IN AMERICA

The conditions associated with people experiencing homelessness have long been understood. Public attention and awareness of homelessness rose in the 1980s and there were two widespread explanations for homelessness that still prevail even today.

According to the Federal Reserve History, the 1981–1982 recession was the worst economic downturn in U.S. history since the Great Depression.[4] This economic condition, of course, gave rise to significant numbers of unemployed individuals, with many facing unsheltered homelessness (Rosenheck 1994[5]). Since then, advocates have emphasized the structural factors that explain homelessness, particularly the availability of affordable housing and of well-paying job opportunities. So, a set of factors explaining the incidence of homelessness include unemployment, economic conditions, and institutional disparities.

A second perspective is much more individualistic and emphasizes the limitations of individuals which then leads them to experience homelessness. For example, the deinstitutionalization of state mental health services left individuals with mental health illness without the proper community level supports and programs. Thus, medical, mental, and

[4] https://www.federalreservehistory.org/essays/recession-of-1981-82.

[5] Homelessness in America. Robert Rosenheck. American Journal of Public Health. December 1994. Volume 84, Edition 12.

substance abuse factors have been linked to individuals experiencing homelessness.

More recently, researchers and practitioners working in the field have identified additional linkages to homelessness, including women and men experiencing domestic violence and racial inequality. Specifically, minority groups in the U.S. experience homelessness at higher rates than other individuals. According to the 2021 Annual Homeless Assessment Report to Congress, Black or African American individuals represented 40.2% of all sheltered individuals.

Multilevel Policies Shaping Homeless Response

Continuum of Care (CoC) Program

Historically, local communities have dealt with the problem of homelessness through the establishment of emergency shelters (Poole and Zugazaga 2003; Opening Doors 2010). While an immediate effort to house homeless people was important, there was recognition that assisting homeless people required a more comprehensive approach that addressed their multidimensional needs. This is because individuals without permanent shelter often are also experiencing physical, emotional, and social problems. As a result, a federal effort to break the cycle of homelessness was established administratively by HUD in 1994 by encouraging the creation of collaborative networks at the local level and providing the resources needed to implement what is known as the Continuum of Care network (HUD 2012). This approach was codified into law in 2009 through the adoption of the HEARTH Act. The idea was that by encouraging the creation of multi-sector networks, the community would have a greater capacity to respond to the incidence of homelessness through the pooling of resources and information and coordination of services to the homeless (i.e., reduce duplication of efforts) (the U.S. Interagency Council on Homelessness 2010).

The CoC program is designed with the intent to achieve collaborative governance as a strategy to reduce or eliminate the incidence of homelessness. Collaborative governance refers to a "a governing arrangement where one or more public agencies directly engage non-state stakeholders in a collective-decision making process that is formal, consensus-oriented, and deliberate and that aims to make or implement public policy or manage public programs or assets" (Ansell and Gash 2008, 544). This intent is evident in several design features of the homeless policy.

First, the policy specifically calls for the active participation of a variety of non-state actors in the homeless network. These non-state actors include homeless service providers, hospitals, advocates, as well as private firms such as affordable housing developers. Public sector agencies encouraged to participate also include public housing agencies, law enforcement, services for veterans, school districts, and mental health agencies. This is different from government (i.e., HUD) attempting to implement homeless programs without engaging critical stakeholders or a lack of collaborative governance.

Second, the policy intends to achieve collaborative governance by allowing the network to be self-organized and to identify its own unique strategy to address problems of homelessness within its community and without requiring leadership by a government entity. Homeless networks, for example, have the freedom to identify a Collaborative Applicant, which HUD recognizes as the entity responsible for applying for HUD's competitive grant process on a yearly basis and overseeing the planning and implementation of homeless programs within the community. This is an important feature because here government is not simply consulting non-state actors but encourages communities to engage in collective decision-making that is formal and consensus-oriented. Thus, any member of the network can take the leading role, including nonprofit organizations. Our work has found that with more frequency, CoC networks are led by Collaborative Applicants that are nonprofit organizations as opposed to local government agencies (see Chapter 2). This means that community members other than government entities are stepping up to the challenge of leading a coalition of providers and advocates to affect positive change. The federal policy also helps achieve collaborative governance by encouraging the network participants to engage in meaningful community work, including developing local strategic plans and work together to conduct yearly counts of sheltered and unsheltered homeless (also referred to as Point-In-Time counts by HUD).

CoC networks are organized to serve almost every corner of the United States (see Table 1.1). There are approximately 421 networks, with some organized to serve rural or statewide areas (9.3%) and others organized to serve local or regional bodies (i.e., city and/or entire county and or/ counties) (90.7%). A vast majority of local or regional CoCs are found in Southeastern and Northeastern states.

Table 1.1 Homeless networks across the United States* by Type ($N = 421$)

Network type	Region of the United States***	Number of networks	Proportion of total networks	Proportion by network type
Statewide	West Coast	5	1.2%	9.3%
	Mountain Plains	14	3.3%	
	Midwest	6	1.4%	
	Southeast	7	1.7%	
	Northeast	7	1.7%	
Local or regional	West Coast	58	13.8%	90.7%
	Mountain Plains	39	9.3%	
	Midwest	72	17.1%	
	Southeast	100	23.8%	
	Northeast	113	26.8%	
	TOTAL	**421**	**100.1%****	**100%**

Notes *Puerto Rico and U.S. territories were excluded. **Total does not equal 100% due to rounding. ***West Coast: Alaska, California, Hawaii, Nevada, Oregon, and Washington. Mountain Plains: Arizona, Arkansas, Colorado, Idaho, Kansas, Montana, Nebraska, New Mexico, North Dakota, Oklahoma, South Dakota, Texas, Utah, and Wyoming. Midwest: Illinois, Indiana, Iowa, Michigan, Minnesota, Missouri, Ohio, and Wisconsin. Southeast: Alabama, Florida, Georgia, Kentucky, Louisiana, Mississippi, North Carolina, South Carolina, Tennessee, Virginia, and West Virginia. Northeast: Connecticut, Delaware, District of Columbia, Maine, Maryland, Massachusetts, New Hampshire, New Jersey, Pennsylvania, Rhode Island, an Vermont
Source HUD Exchange

At the local level, these CoCs are often labeled as coalitions or community partnerships on homelessness. For example, the CoC serving Salt Lake City/County is named the Salt Lake Valley Coalition to End Homelessness[6] and it relies on funding from HUD's CoC program as well as resources from state agencies and local philanthropic groups (see Fig. 1.3). And a CoC that serves Dallas county and Collin county in Texas (TX-600) is led by a nonprofit organization named Metro Dallas Homeless Alliance (MDHA).[7] MDHA is a stand-alone nonprofit organization that represents TX-600 CoC and is responsible for coordinating housing and supportive services for homeless individuals and families. It is common for a CoC network to have a different name and to be a part of larger community efforts.

[6] https://endutahhomelessness.org/salt-lake-valley/.

[7] https://www.mdhadallas.org/.

WHO WE ARE

The Salt Lake Valley Coalition to End Homelessness (SLVCEH) is committed to rendering homelessness brief, rare and non-recurring, in collaboration with our statewide homeless service partners within the Utah Homelessness Network. Members of the coalition aim to achieve this vision by:

1. Identifying gaps in the system;

2. Utilizing data, research and resources to establish creative, effective strategies to address gaps;

3. Supporting, informing, and collaborating on funding; educating the public and stakeholders regarding homelessness prevention and solutions.

We are working tirelessly to move individuals experiencing homelessness into long-term stable housing by addressing the core needs of individuals experiencing homelessness through our eight Core Function Groups.

Fig. 1.3 Salt lake city/county continuum of care network (UT-500)

The benefits of communities creating CoC networks are many. First, communities can access federal funds through the yearly competition of CoC funding allocated by Congress. Second, CoCs have access to technical assistance and guidance from HUD through the CoC program. For example, HUD provided COVID-19 resources for homeless providers including webinars, vaccine updates, and other critical information. Lastly, by creating a network, communities are able to pool local resources as well and develop coordinated plans to address homelessness in their community as opposed to working in silos.

Federal Strategic Plan

While HUD through the CoC program attempts to provide direction and technical guidance to homeless networks at the local level, the U.S. Interagency Council on Homelessness (USICH)[8] works to implement broader

---

[8] https://www.usich.gov/.

federal strategies to end homelessness in the United States. It is acknowledged as the only federal agency with the sole mission of addressing homelessness through a council comprised of 19 federal agencies. This council is charged with creating and implementing the Federal Strategic Plan to Prevent and End Homelessness. Current strategies supported by USICH include:

1. Housing—developing strategies that get people housed through a Housing First approach;
2. Integrate Health Care—recognizing that often people experiencing homelessness are also experiencing a health care and/or behavioral health need(s);
3. Build Career Pathways—people experiencing homelessness need an increased access to sustainable and well-paying jobs;
4. Foster Education Connections—children and youth need continued access to the education system, which can provide safety and a network of support;
5. Strengthen Crisis Response Systems—coordinated entry and facilitating quick connection to rapid housing and permanent shelter solutions to reduce the traumatic effects of homelessness;
6. Reduce Criminal Justice Involvement—data suggests a connection between streets, shelters, and jails;
7. Build Partnerships—solutions to homelessness require that community providers and advocates come together to develop cohesive solutions;
8. Prevent Homelessness—working to prevent homelessness by reducing risks and addressing housing needs and stability.

During the COVID-19 pandemic, USICH worked with federal partners and beyond to identify strategies to contain the spread and develop best practices to address COVID-19 infection among people experiencing homelessness. For example, USICH collaborated with the Centers for Disease Control (CDC) to develop operational guidance and protocols based on science for front-line homeless service providers.

State Priorities

In addition to federal policies and programs, states and local governments have opportunities to implement and re-shape priorities for their constituencies. While some states have state-level strategic plans, many do not. Common strategies in state-level plans include efforts such as: increasing housing options for homeless people, improving coordinated entry into the homeless service system, and increasing funds for homeless programs. For example, the State of Utah Strategic Plan on Homelessness identifies the goals of working together to: (1) make homelessness rare, (2) make homelessness brief, (3) make homelessness non-recurring, (4) collaborate across the sectors, and (5) address homelessness in all of Utah. The plan specifically identifies 5-year performance goals in four HUD system performance measures:

1. Fewer days spent in emergency beds or shelters;
2. Fewer persons returning to homelessness;
3. Fewer first-time individuals who experience homelessness;
4. More persons successfully retaining housing.

Additionally, the plan identifies critical gaps in the homeless service system that the state as a whole must address in order to achieve success in the preceding performance measures. The gaps identified by the plan include:

1. Affordable housing, permanent supportive housing, and emergency beds;
2. Mental health services and substance use disorder treatment;
3. Case management;
4. Prevention, diversion, and outreach services;
5. Data systems that capture more of the full story;
6. Available transportation.

In Table 1.2, we identify samples of statewide plans. States with a high concentration of homelessness (i.e., California, New York, and Texas) have statewide plan of addressing homelessness and provide fund in support of homelessness. The State of California, which has the highest homeless population in the country, has led rehousing services during the COVID-19 pandemic.

Table 1.2   Examples of statewide strategic plans

State	Website of strategic plan
Alaska	https://www.ahfc.us/application/files/6615/4905/0609/ach_progress_report_2018.pdf
California	https://www.cdss.ca.gov/inforesources/cdss-programs/housing-programs/project-roomkey
Colorado	https://www.coloradocoalition.org/sites/default/files/2020-03/Strategic%20Plan%202020_final.pdf
Hawaii	https://homelessness.hawaii.gov/wp-content/uploads/2022/03/HICH-Ten-Year-Plan-Draft-Document-For-PIG-Review-Rev-03-04-22.pdf
New York	https://hcr.ny.gov/system/files/documents/2019/09/2020%20Action%20Plan-%20Public%20Comment%20Draft.pdf
Texas	https://www.tdhca.state.tx.us/tich/pathways-home.htm
Utah	https://jobs.utah.gov/homelessness/homelessnessstrategicplan.pdf

REFERENCES

Ansell, Chris, and Alison Gash. 2008. Collaborative Governance in Theory and Practice. *Journal of Public Administration Research & Theory* 18 (4): 543–571.

Poole, Dennis L., and Carole B. Zugazaga. 2003. Conceptualizing Prevention as the First Line of Offense against Homelessness: Implications for the Federal Continuum of Care Model. *Journal of Primary Prevention* 23 (4): 409–424.

Rosenheck, R. 1994. Homelessness in America. *American Journal of Public Health* 84 (12): 1885–1886.

The Homeless Emergency Assistance and Rapid Transition to Housing Act 2009 (HEARTH). S. 896 (US).

The U.S. Department of Housing and Urban Development. 2012. *Establishing and Operating a CoC.*

The U.S. Department of Housing and Urban Development. 2020. *The 2020 Annual Homeless Assessment Report (AHAR) to Congress.*

The U.S. Department of Housing and Urban Development. 2021. *Education for Homeless Children and Youths (EHCY) Program CFDA 84.196.*

The U.S. Interagency Council on Homelessness. 2010. *Opening Doors: Federal Strategic Plan to Prevent and End Homelessness.* Washington, DC: U. S. Government Printing Office.

CHAPTER 2

Designing Collaboration Networks and the Role of Nonprofit Organizations

Abstract Cross-sector collaboration has become either an expected or required governance form to effectively resolve wicked problems that cannot be addressed by a single organization. This chapter presents the design of CoC networks as collaborative bodies and offers a detailed description on the number and type of CoC networks and the jurisdictions they serve. This chapter utilizes case study data of CoC networks and presents details of the variety of cross-sector actors involved in the collaboration process, and the prominent leadership role that nonprofit organizations play in collaborative governance.

Keywords Cross-sector collaboration · Collaborative applicant · Nonprofit organizations

Continuum of Care (CoC) homeless networks are the primary homeless service units in local communities. CoCs play a key role in bringing stakeholders together, creating local strategic plans, implementing programs and initiatives, and consolidating funding needs into a single grant application to HUD on behalf of their locality. But how are these CoC networks designed? Who leads and who joins the network? This chapter presents a detailed description on the number and type of CoC networks

H. S. Jang and J. N. Valero, *Public-Nonprofit Collaboration and Policy in Homeless Services*, https://doi.org/10.1007/978-3-031-11918-7_2

and the jurisdictions they serve. Using a case study of CoC networks within a region of the United States, we also review the variety of cross-sector actors involved in the collaboration process.

Cross-sector collaboration has become either an expected or required form of governance to effectively resolve wicked problems that cannot be addressed by a single organization. Public organizations are increasingly dependent on nonprofit and private organizations because of the benefits embedded in collaborative networks such as access to resources, cost benefits, and the opportunity to access the local expertise. As discussed earlier, the HEARTH Act of 2009 established the Continuum of Care program and HUD developed and published the CoC program interim rule in 2012 to develop a community-based service network. Since the implementation of the HEARTH Act, HUD requires communities to establish a local CoC network to bring cross-sector providers together. The CoC network is expected to develop a community commitment to end homelessness by connecting government and nonprofit stakeholders and service providers. CoC networks are a locally driven approach in service of people experiencing homeless with an expectation that each community develops its service approach and develops programs based on the unique conditions of the homeless population and local strengths and challenges within the community. This CoC program was proposed as a service structure that consistently evolves in order to tailor approaches and strategies to the unique needs and challenges of the local homeless population.

Local communities, therefore, create CoC networks in order to carry out the purposes of the CoC program, and HUD has identified several key responsibilities of CoCs. Under the HEARTH Act of 2009, the HUD CoC program interim rule[1] codifies the eligibility and responsibilities of CoCs. Figure 2.1 presents a summary of CoCs' responsibilities.

The federal policy allows for CoC networks to create its own membership with a wide array of program design and administrative arrangements. For example, a local CoC covers diverse types of geographical districts including a city, a county, cities, counties, or a combination of counties and cities or an entire state.

---

[1] https://www.hudexchange.info/resource/2033/hearth-coc-program-interim-rule/.

I.   Submit a single application that consolidates three homeless assistance programs: Supportive Housing Program, the Shelter Plus Program, and the Moderate Rehabilitation/Single Room Occupancy (SRO) Program.

II. Promote and manage community-wide planning: CoC is required to be a leading role in the local planning process in the development of the Consolidated Plan to the HUD funding application.

III. Improve data collection process: CoC is leading the entire process of the annual Point in time (PIT) counts and responsible to develop and manage the Homeless Management Information System (HMIS). CoC collects client-level data by creating and managing Coordinated Data Entry System and measures their performance to this system.

IV. Develop performance measurement and report progress: CoCs are required to report progress to HUD as a key competitive component of HUD funding application. CoCs are expected to develop performance data and successfully submit them to System Performance Measures data.

V.   Develop strategies for effective use of resources: CoCs are managing coordinated entry of homeless-related data collection and sharing data to service entities.

VI. Develop emergency transfer plan: CoCs are required to formulate the emergency transitional plan under the requirements.

Fig. 2.1 Eligibility and Responsibilities of CoCs (*Source* HUD CoC program interim rule)

Collaborative Applicants: CoC Leading Agencies

According to the CoC federal interim rule, the Continuum of Care network is responsible for designating an agency to assume the role of Collaborative Applicant, which is the only entity allowed to apply for a CoC program grant from HUD on behalf of the CoC network (HUD 2012). Here, the Collaborative Applicant functions as the lead agency responsible for soliciting funding applications from network members, submitting a single application, and overseeing the administration of the funded projects and other collaborative activities.

CoC program interim rule notes that eligible applicants include nonprofit organizations, state and city and county agencies, and public housing authorities. An applicant has to be designated as a "Collaborative Applicant" by the CoC in the submission of a funding application and this Collaborative Applicant is responsible for overseeing program implementation and submitting an application for funding to HUD.

Table 2.1 shows the cross-sector representation of Collaborative Applicants. As shown, CoCs networks are led by nonprofits, city, county, or

Table 2.1 Local CoC collaborative applicants leadership (N = 346)

Collaborative applicant	Number of networks	Proportion from total networks (%)
Nonprofit	166	48.0
City	26	7.5
County	73	21.1
State	3	0.9
Coalition	78	22.5
	346	100

Source HUD Exchange Website

partnership of cross-sector agencies. There are also cases where the CoC is led by a partnership, coalition, regional commission, or consulting firm.

ROLE OF NONPROFIT ORGANIZATIONS IN CoC HOMELESS NETWORKS

As shown in Table 2.1, about half of the CoCs that are locally developed are led by nonprofit organizations followed by 21% of county and 7.5% of city agencies. In about 22.5% of cases, networks are led by coalitions of entities partnering together to provide CoC leadership, often including a nonprofit entity as a key partner. This shows that nonprofits are not only participating in the collaboration process as expected by the federal interim rule, but they are also assuming an important role by leading other organizations in the quest to eradicate homelessness within their community. It is noteworthy that many of nonprofit leading CoCs have established an independent 501(c)(3) public charity for the effective operation of the CoC programs. This means that some networks have evolved into a more structured form of governance (which is further discussed in Chapter 3). Nonprofit organizations are in a good position to take on the leading role in CoC homeless networks for reasons that are centered on the nature of the nonprofit sector.

First and foremost, because nonprofit organizations tend to be community based and focused on helping their specific locality, nonprofits are likely to have established legitimacy and trust with other community organizations (Ott and Dicke 2021; Wolf 1999). As such, nonprofits are positioned to lead the process of activating key members of a network and initiating the collaboration process (O'Regan and Oster 2000; Wolch

1990). Activation is a crucial first step in collaborative governance where a lead organization, such as a human service nonprofit, identifies potential members of a network who are needed to achieve program goals and actively pursues their cooperation and membership (Agranoff and McGuire 2001; McGuire 2002). In a study of perceived effectiveness of an emergency manager's network, McGuire and Silvia (2009) found that although activation was not a statistically significant predictor of network effectiveness, "it was the leadership behavior that was engaged in most often" (53). Activation is a key component of the collaboration process, in which nonprofits are positioned to achieve because of their tendency to have established relationships with community stakeholders.

Second, a service network led by a nonprofit will not be perceived as a government entity to potential funders and can establish itself as a public charity; hence, a nonprofit-led network will be in a better position to mobilize support and secure a variety of private financial resources including: grants, gifts/contributions, membership dues, income from special fundraising events, program service fees, and/or contracts. A nonprofit's access to these private resources matters because it creates opportunities for nonprofits to secure needed resources for collaborative efforts. Nonprofits can also pursue social media giving campaigns in the form of gifts/contributions, which tend to carry less oversight (when compared to government grants) on how they are spent and can be accordingly used for collaborative activities (Kanter and Paine 2012). Some nonprofits even turn to entrepreneurial activities for purposes of acquiring additional funding sources and achieving higher levels of service to a community (Jung et al. 2016; Young 1998). Unlike their government counterparts who tend to rely on legislative allocations with strict oversight on how the public funding is used (Rosen 1998), nonprofits are thus uniquely positioned to lead a network because of their ability to mobilize and secure private funding resources that are useful and necessary to advance the goals of the collaborative arrangement.

Third, as in hierarchy, leading a network requires selling a mission and vision to collaborative partners and other stakeholders, which is important for providing a sense of direction and purpose for the collaborative process. Nonprofit organizations tend to be characterized as mission-oriented and focused on addressing a particular cause without concern for monetary profit (Eng et al. 2012; Frumkin 2002) and as such, are positioned to lead a collaborative network because of their natural capacity to frame a vision and mission and build consensus among network stakeholders. Nonprofits tend to be well connected to the community they serve and to have established relationships with community leaders, which translate into established trust with third parties. In addition, nonprofit organizations are known to be strong advocates for their causes (Almog-Bar and Schmid 2014); thus, nonprofits have the capacity to build support for collaborative efforts among key community stakeholders.

From a government perspective, nonprofits are also positioned to take on leading role in human service networks for a number of reasons. Nonprofits, for instance, can easily mobilize volunteers for collaborative activities. Volunteers are an important human resource that can be leveraged for collaborative efforts when the use of volunteers produces benefits such as cost savings, increased capacity of nonprofit, and expert knowledge. The use of volunteers can also help raise public awareness and support of collaborative activities when through their volunteer work, citizens learn about the needs and challenges of the community and efforts of the collaborative arrangement (Brudney and Kellough 2000). Public service networks, thus, are afforded an opportunity to leverage on the flexibility and resources, such as volunteers, available to the nonprofit sector to advance collaborative efforts aimed at achieving public outcomes.

Nonprofits can also pursue partnerships with faith-based organizations and religious congregations without political concerns or the stigma of meshing church and state relations. Ebaugh et al. (2007), for example, find that faith-based organizations are more likely to collaborate with other faith-based and mainstream nonprofit organizations than with government entities. Government, therefore, can leverage from nonprofit-led networks to secure the partnership of faith-based organizations in the collaboration process.

Government organizations benefit from nonprofit leading networks because nonprofits are community based and they tend to have a better grasp on the needs of the locality. U.S. government organizations have a vested interest in ensuring that public services are responsive to the needs of the community. In the case of federal homeless policy, HUD has specifically encouraged local communities to address the incidence of homelessness through local collaboration because the incidence of homelessness varies, as do the resources and capacities of communities. Nonprofits tend to develop expertise in their service areas, and as such, government benefits from not having to reinvent the wheel. Nonprofit-led collaboration, therefore, increases government's ability to ensure that the needs and interests of local communities are well understood and represented in collaborative efforts.

Lastly, governments are by nature risk-averse and dealing with homelessness is fraught with risks. Thus, governments are protected from criticism but can still enjoy the benefits of program experimentation when nonprofits lead.

MEMBERSHIP OF CoC PROGRAM

The CoC program is connecting key community stakeholders and engaging them in homeless services as members of CoC. The member agencies and individuals do not have to be a funded entity in most of the cases and those entities represent diverse service areas including health and human services, services for the veterans, criminal justice, and government agencies. In Table 2.2, a descriptive review of 35 CoC networks within a Mountain Plains region of the United States was identified, which includes the States of Arizona, Arkansas, Colorado, Idaho, Kansas, Montana, Nebraska, New Mexico, North Dakota, Oklahoma, South Dakota, Texas, Utah, and Wyoming. The purpose of identifying a single region was to collect more in-depth information on the organizational membership of homeless networks.

Analysis of 1,542 organizations which are member organizations of 35 CoC networks in Mountain Plains region resulted in the identification of 11 types of organizations, which include: city government, county government, state government, court system, federal government, nonprofit, faith-based nonprofit, church, school district, university, individual citizens, and business organizations. These organizations are further categorized based on sector orientations such as public (i.e., city, county, state, court), nonprofit (i.e., mainstream nonprofit, faith-based nonprofit, church), education (i.e., school district, university), private (i.e., business), and unknown (i.e., for those organizations that sector was not identified). Results indicate that the nonprofit sector accounts for a vast majority of the membership of local CoC networks, with 68% of total organizations being a nonprofit, faith-based, or church organization. Within the nonprofit sector, the majority of organizations tend to be mainstream nonprofits, followed by faith-based organizations and then religious congregations.

Table 2.2 Local homeless network member composition for the Mountain Plains region[2]

Sector	Type of organization	Total number	Proportion by category (%)	Proportion by sector (%)
Public	City	169	11	20.9
	County	84	5.5	
	State	62	4	
	Court system	2	0.1	
	Federal	5	0.3	
Nonprofit	Nonprofit	816	52.9	68.2
	Faith-based nonprofit	201	13	
	Church[a]	34	2.2	
Education	School district	62	4	5.6
	University	24	1.6	
Private	Individual citizens	24	1.6	4.9
	Business organizations	51	3.3	
Other	Unknown	8	0.5	0.5
	Total	**1542**	**100**	**100.1[b]**

Notes [a]Organizations that provided health and/or human services and were associated to a religion were coded as faith-based, whereas organized religions were coded as churches
[b]Total does not equal 100% due to rounding

Economic theories of government failure and market failure as well as transaction cost and contract failure theories suggest that nonprofits tend to be the deliverer of public services (Salamon 1987; Smith and Lipsky 1993; Young 1998), and homeless services seem to not be the exception. In addition, nonprofits are also likely motivated to take membership in these networks and collaborate with other organizations on the issue of homeless services because of the reasons related to resource dependency (Pfeffer and Salancik 1978), institutional pressure to participate (DiMaggio and Powell 1983), and/or network embeddedness (Guo and Acar 2005). The public sector, on the other hand, accounted for

---

[2] Mountain Plains region includes the following states: Arizona, Arkansas, Colorado, Idaho, Kansas, Montana, Nebraska, New Mexico, North Dakota, Oklahoma, South Dakota, Texas, Utah, and Wyoming.

about 21% of the membership of these 25 homeless networks, while the education and private sectors accounted for 6% and 4%, respectively.

Overall, these results indicate that nonprofit organizations play a prominent role in the implementation of federal homeless policy. In addition, this variety of non-state actors suggests that the federal policy is achieving some level of success in its collaborative governance intent. Achieving broad inclusion of stakeholders in the collaborative process matters because it helps pool a wide range of necessary resources to address the multidimensional needs of homeless people (Milward and Provan 2006; Opening Doors 2010).

REFERENCES

Agranoff, Robert, and Michael McGuire. 2001. Big Questions in Public Network Management Research. *Journal of Public Administration Research and Theory* 11 (3): 295–326.

Almog-Bar, Michal, and Hillel Schmid. 2014. Advocacy Activities of Nonprofit Human Service Organizations: A Critical Review. *Nonprofit and Voluntary Sector Quarterly* 43 (1): 11–35.

Brudney, Jeffrey L., and J. Edward Kellough. 2000. Volunteers in State Government: Involvement, Management, and Benefits. *Nonprofit and Voluntary Sector Quarterly* 29 (1): 111–130.

DiMaggio, Paul J., and Walter W. Powell. 1983. The Iron Cage Revisited: Institutional Isomorphism and Collective Rationality in Organizational Fields. *American Sociological Review* 48 (2): 147–160.

Ebaugh, Helen Rose, Janet S. Chafetz, and Paula F. Pipes. 2007. Collaborations with Faith-Based Social Service Coalitions. *Nonprofit Management and Leadership* 18 (2): 175–191.

Eng, Teck-Yong, Chih-Yao Gordon Liu, and Yasmin Kaur Sekhon. 2012. The Role of Relationally Embedded Network Ties in Resource Acquisition of British Nonprofit Organizations. *Nonprofit and Voluntary Sector Quarterly* 41 (6): 1092–1115.

Frumkin, Peter. 2002. *On Being Nonprofit*. Cambridge, MA: Harvard University Press.

Guo, Chao, and Muhittin Acar. 2005. Understanding Collaboration Among Nonprofit Organizations: Combining Resource Dependency, Institutional, and Network Perspectives. *Nonprofit and Voluntary Sector Quarterly* 34 (3): 340–361.

Jung, Kyujin, Hee Soun Jang, and Inseok Seo. 2016. Government-Driven Social Enterprises in South Korea: Lessons from the Social Enterprise Promotion

Program in the Seoul Metropolitan Government. *International Review & Administrative Sciences* 82 (3): 598–616.

Kanter, Beth, and Katie Delahaye Paine. 2012. *Measuring the Networked Nonprofit: Using Data to Change the World.* Hoboken: Wiley.

McGuire, Michael. 2002. Managing Networks: Propositions on What Managers Do and Why They Do It. *Public Administration Review* 62 (5): 599–609.

McGuire, Michael, and Chris Silvia. 2009. Does Leadership in Networks Matter? Examining the Effect of Leadership Behaviors on Managers' Perceptions of Network Effectiveness. *Public Performance and Management Review* 33 (1): 34–62.

Milward, H. Brinton, and Keith G. Provan. 2006. *A Manager's Guide to Choosing and Using Collaborative Networks.* Washington, DC: IBM Center for the Business Government.

O'Regan, Katherine M., and Sharon M. Oster. 2000. Nonprofit and for-Profit Partnerships: Rationale and Challenges of Cross-Sector Contracting. *Nonprofit and Voluntary Sector Quarterly* 29 (1): 120–140.

Ott, Steve, and Lisa A. Dicke. 2021. *The Nature of the Nonprofit Sector.* New York, NY: Routledge.

Pfeffer, Jeffrey, and Gerald R. Salancik. 1978. *The External Control of Organizations: A Resource Dependence Perspective.* New York: Harper & Row.

Rosen, Bernard. 1998. *Holding Government Bureaucracies Accountable.* Westport: Praeger.

Salamon, Lester M. 1987. Of Market Failure, Voluntary Failure, and Third-Party Government: Toward a Theory of Government-Nonprofit Relations in the Modern Welfare State. *Journal of Voluntary Action Research* 16 (1–2): 29–49.

Smith, Steven Rathgeb, and Michael Lipsky. 1993. *Nonprofits for Hire.* Cambridge, MA: Harvard University Press.

The Homeless Emergency Assistance and Rapid Transition to Housing: Continuum of Care Program; Interim Final Rule, 2506-AC29 C.F.R. 2012.

The Homeless Emergency Assistance and Rapid Transition to Housing Act 2009 (HEARTH). S. 896 (US).

The U.S. Department of Housing and Urban Development. 2012. *Establishing and Operating a CoC.*

The U.S. Interagency Council on Homelessness. 2010. *Opening Doors: Federal Strategic Plan to Prevent and End Homelessness.* Washington, DC: U.S. Government Printing Office.

Wolch, Jennifer R. 1990. Homelessness in America. *Journal of Urban Affairs* 12 (4): 449–463.

Wolf, Thomas. 1999. *Managing a Nonprofit Organization: Updated Twenty-First-Century Edition.* New York, NY: Free Press.

Young, Dennis R. 1998. Commercialism in Nonprofit Social Service Associations: Its Character, Significance, and Rationale. *Journal of Public Analysis and Management* 17 (2): 278–297.

CHAPTER 3

Managing Collaborations and the Network Governance

Abstract To be effective in pooling resources and addressing the incidence of homelessness, CoC networks like other types of collaborative arrangements need to be managed effectively. This chapter offers a comprehensive discussion on the management of CoC networks and discusses the role of non-state actors in leading and managing public service networks. Using Provan and Kenis' (Journal of Public Administration Research and Theory 25: 479–511, 2008) network governance framework, we categorize CoCs' network governance forms and discuss key factors that affect CoCs' form of governance.

Keywords Network governance · Shared governance · Lead organization · Network administrative organization (NAO)

Collaborations require effective management in order to produce intended results, and in the case of homeless networks, that means pooling resources to address the Continuum of Care needs of people experiencing homelessness and ultimately reducing the incidence of homelessness. This chapter offers a comprehensive discussion on the management of CoC networks. Management of collaboration requires a

Table 3.1 Features of an organization vs. network

Dimension	Organization	Network
Sectoral nature	Single sector	Cross-sector organizations
Legal nature	Legally registered entity	May not be a legally registered entity
Governance	Defined decision-making mechanisms	Evolving decision-making mechanisms
Membership	Employed, with assigned positions and duties	Autonomous and independent participants
Accountability	Documented rules that hold members accountable	Understood norms and shared expectations among autonomous members

specific skillset which is different from those involved in managing a single organization.

There are meaningful differences between managing a collaboration and managing a single entity. Organizations represent a single sector (i.e., public, private, or nonprofit), whereas a collaborative network is comprised of cross-sector organizations. Organizations also tend to be legally registered entities with defined decision-making mechanisms and documented rules that hold employees and volunteers accountable, whereas networks may not be legally registered entities and tend to have evolving decision-making mechanisms in place with understood norms and shared expectations among autonomous members. These key differences demand a different management approach to collaborations (see Table 3.1).

In their study of emergency managers, Silvia and McGuire (2010)[1] find that there are meaningful differences in how managers approach leadership within their organization when compared to how they approach leadership within their network. Specifically, managers tended to use more people-oriented behaviors such as *treating all as equals, creating trust*, and *sharing leadership role* within their network settings. While managing their organization, on the other hand, managers used task-oriented behaviors more frequently such as *scheduling the work to be done* and *assigning particular tasks*. In this chapter, we explore the governance

[1] "Leading public sector networks: An empirical examination of integrative leadership behaviors." *Leadership Quarterly* (2010).

and management of homeless networks with particular attention to the arrangements that these collaborations pursue to govern their affairs and the key management behaviors that are prominently reported by homeless network leaders.

NETWORK GOVERNANCE

Thomson and Perry (2006) note that organizations working together must come to some consensus on how their work together will be governed. Governance is about the rules and structures that network members as autonomous organizations will apply in order to make joint decisions about their community efforts for collective outcome, including things such as dispersing and allocating funds to specific programs, deciding which initiatives to pursue, and addressing conflict when it arises. Although the form of network governance is not a common topic of discussion in the network and collaboration literature, it is a relevant and key topic to the cases where the collaboration involves organizations working together to advance a public effort and/or use of public resources. Network governance is a specific set of rules that set boundaries of actions, accountabilities, responsibilities, and stabilities of network operation and coordination (Torfing 2005; Sorensen and Torfing 2005). In the case of CoC homeless networks, establishing a governance arrangement is critical to the ethical and accountable use of federal, state, and local funds and other resources used to tackle the challenges surrounding homeless policy. As such, the HUD interim rule[2] governing these networks sets expectations for how a CoC board must be structured:

- Be representative of the relevant organizations and of projects serving homeless subpopulations;
- Include at least one homeless or formerly homeless individual.

In addition to this structural requirement, the interim rule lays out a number of responsibilities that the CoC network and their board must comply with (see Fig. 3.1).

Although all of CoCs have to create a board to manage matters of network, the HUD interim rule does not provide additional guidance

---

[2] Section 578.5(b).

- Hold meetings of the full membership, with published agendas, at least semi-annually;
- Make an invitation for new members to join publicly available within the geographic at least annually;
- Adopt and follow a written process to select a board to act on behalf of the Continuum of Care. The process must be reviewed, updated, and approved by the Continuum at least once every 5 years;
- Appoint additional committees, subcommittees, or workgroups.

Fig. 3.1 Responsibilities of CoC networks and their boards

detailing the specific governance structure that the network must comply with. In other words, CoC networks may design and determine their own way of governing within responsibilities of networks. The choice of specific governance structure is important for decision-making, communication, and membership of HUD-funded and non-funded agencies. Not only CoC homeless service networks, governance of network has been discussed as critical to development, sustainability, and success of social and human service networks (Cristofoli et al. 2014; Raab et al. 2013; Mosley and Jarpe 2019; Park and Park 2009). A network governance that is shared among members of collaborative services will engage members as active co-producers of services and lead policy actors and key stakeholders to contribute community commitment in achieving positive network outcome. Governance in the networked settings has both formal and informal dimensions and even those documented network governances are evolving as a network grows or changes its operations. In some cases, management of CoC and decision-making is highly formalized but many CoCs updating charter and operating rules as needed.

Diverse types of network governances are used in CoC homeless service networks and their choice of governance links actors from cross sectors and cross industries and shifts power dynamics among members. Not all network governances are alike. Provan and Kenis (2008) describe network governance is a strategic choice of network participants to generate positive collective outcome and delineate three different types of network governance. We use this framework of Provan and Kenis to categorize CoC's choices of network governance as listed below:

- Shared governance;
- Lead organization;
- Network administrative organization (NAO).

Shared governance involves members of a network all engaging deeply in the affairs of the collaboration through either informal or formal means. In this form of governance, there is no specific entity or group within the collaboration in charge of governing with defined authority. Instead, all needs of the network are addressed in a collective forum with all network members or by a board which represents the entire body of network members. This means that all members are equally responsible for managing both internal and external relationships and thus requires the active commitment from each.

Lead organization form of governance is more centralized form of control compared with shared governance form. A single agency of the network is responsible for leading the collaboration, managing its internal affairs, and coordinating community efforts and relationships. This lead organization is still a member of the network who is often a longtime service provider in the community and well respected by community organizations. In a lead organization form of governance, the organization in charge of administration and coordination of activities may receive additional financial resources from the network to compensate their administrative efforts for network operation. For example, CoC program funding allows for homeless networks to apply for administrative funding. It is also a common case that the leading agency shares its administrative capacity in support of network, especially if the network is in its development stage or the network is rather small with limited members and resources.

When a collaboration or a service network chooses to develop a completely separate entity to govern the affairs and activities of the collaboration, it has a network administrative organization (NAO) as a form of governance. While no current member of the collaboration is designated to lead, members still play an active role via membership, board membership, and service in committees and/or workgroups. Compared to lead organization form, still the decision-making structure is centralized in NAO network governance. This form of governance involves a NAO focused exclusively on network administration only without any service function carried in the community. There is also a hybrid form of NAO in which the NAO provides services on top of their administrative responsibility to lead and manage CoC network. Often those hybrid CoCs offer services that are focused on community-wide efforts such as capacity-building and fundraising and resource allocation. Thus, this

Table 3.2   Governance structures of CoC homeless networks

Governance structures	Number	Percent
Shared governance	76	40
Lead organization	56	30
Network Administrative Organization (NAO)	NAO—32 (17%)	40
	Service NAO—25 (13%)	
Total	189	100

hybrid type of network governance is called Service Network Administrative Organization (SNAO). The development of the NAO as a separate entity often comes at the decision of the network as a whole and can be established as a stand-alone nonprofit organization whose sole mission is to lead CoC.

In 2018, a national survey of CoC homeless networks informs that a majority of network respondents (40%) are governed through the shared governance model, meaning that all members share equality in the management of collaboration's affairs (see Table 3.2). The lead organization model is the next common form with 30% of all networks responding to our survey. Including service NAOs, 40% of CoC networks are managed by a stand-alone organization that manages CoC coordination and service operations.

For example, the Dallas City & County/Irving Continuum of Care Network (TX-600) is led by a stand-alone nonprofit organization, Metro Dallas Homeless Alliance (MDHA). MDHA is the CoC's network administrative organization (NAO) that is responsible for providing administrative support and guidance to more than 90 cross-sector agencies in Dallas and Collin counties (see Fig. 3.2).

FACTORS ASSOCIATED WITH FORM OF GOVERNANCE

Complex policy issues such as homelessness are easy to face collective action problems or the unwillingness of individual organizations to cooperate and work with others. Organizations stretched thin with limited resources and with high competition for available funding opportunities may easily choose to focus on their own individual organization needs as opposed to focusing on working across boundaries. To reduce potential collective action problems, some homeless networks may choose to

The Metro Dallas Homeless Alliance (MDHA)

The **Metro Dallas Homeless Alliance (MDHA)** is a backbone organization that leads the development of an effective homeless rehousing system. In partnership with 90+ public, private, and nonprofit institutions, we make the experience of homelessness in Dallas and Collin Counties rare, brief, and non-recurring.

Research shows that no one organization can do this alone. A collective impact approach is a must. Collective impact requires a **strong backbone organization**, like MDHA, with subject matter expertise, "the skills and resources to assemble and coordinate the specific elements necessary," and the ability to handle "the myriad logistical and administrative details needed," to reach shared goals.

In its landmark legislation on homelessness, the 2009 Homeless Emergency Assistance and Rapid Transition to Housing (HEARTH) Act, and in Opening Doors, the original Federal strategic plan to end homelessness, established under the Act, Congress mandated that there be a homeless rehousing system (or Continuum of Care) in every community, each with a designated lead agency. In Dallas and Collin Counties the Continuum of Care is known as the **Homeless Collaborative**, and **MDHA** is its designated lead agency.

Fig. 3.2 Metro Dallas Homeless Alliance as NAO (Network Administrative Organization) example (*Source* https://www.mdhadallas.org/mdha/)

adopt the NAO model in order to outsource the work of managing the collaborative efforts to a single entity formed to manage their collaborative affairs. This means creating a stand-alone organization that is solely focused on managing system-wide efforts.

A recent dissertation study reviewed the key factors that may affect CoC's NAO form of governance rather than either shared governance or lead organization forms, and tested degree to which problem severity, network capacity, and nonprofit capacity explained a network's choice to adopt the NAO form of governance (Jeong 2021). Research reports that homeless problem severity, as measured by number of veteran homeless, and network capacity, as measured by permanent housing units available, are positively associated with adoption of NAO form of governance. However, an increase in the amount of federal funding is negatively associated with NAO governance—meaning that networks with more federal homeless funding are more like to choose a shared governance or lead organization model of governance. According to these findings, home-less networks are more likely to reduce uncertainty and risks by adopting NAO form of governance when the homeless problem is severe requiring a centralized and professionalized management of CoC network.

REFERENCES

Cristofoli, D., J. Markovic, and M. Meneguzzo. 2014. Governance, Manage-ment and Performance in Public Networks: How to Be Successful in Shared-Governance Networks. *Journal of Management & Governance* 18 (1): 77–93.

Jeong, J. 2021. The Study of Network Governance in Continuum of Care Homeless Service Networks in the U.S: Institutional Collective Action Frame-work. Doctoral dissertation, University of North Texas (Open Access Disserta-tion). https://oatd.org/oatd/record?record=info:ark%2F67531%2Fmetadc1 873856.

Mosley, J.E., and M. Jarpe. 2019. How Structural Variations in Collaborative Governance Networks Influence Advocacy Involvement and Outcomes. *Public Administration Review* 79 (5): 629–640.

Park, H.J., and M.J. Park. 2009. Types of Network Governance and Network Performance: Community Development Project Case. *International Review of Public Administration* 13 (s1): 91–105.

Provan, Keith G., and Patrick Kenis. 2008. Modes of Network Governance: Structure, Management, and Effectiveness. *Journal of Public Administration Research and Theory* 18 (2): 229–252.

Raab, J., R.S. Mannak, and B. Cambre. 2013. Combining Structure, Gover-nance, and Context: A Configurational Approach to Network Effectiveness. *Journal of Public Administration Research and Theory* 25 (2): 479–511.

Silvia, Chris, and Michael McGuire. 2010. Leading Public Sector Networks: An Empirical Examination of Integrative Leadership Behaviors. *The Leadership Quarterly* 21 (2): 264–277.

Sorensen, E., and J. Torfing. 2005. The Democratic Anchorage of Governance Networks. *Scandinavian Political Studies* 28 (3): 195–218.

Thomson, Ann Marie, and James L. Perry. 2006. Collaboration Processes: Inside the Black Box. *Public Administration Review* 66 (s1): 20–32.

Torfing, J. 2005. Governance Network Theory: Towards a Second Generation. *European Political Science* 4 (3): 305–315.

CHAPTER 4

Collaborative Leadership and Individual Champions

Abstract A leader in collaboration has to maintain high ethical standards and be a strong role model in order for members of the network to accept network vision and goals through their idealized influence. This chapter reviews the leadership literature in the context of cross-sector collaboration and discusses the important role that individual leadership plays within CoC networks. To examine leadership behavior of CoC leaders, we adopt Bass and Avolio's (Multifactor leadership questionnaire: Manual and sample set. Mind Garden, Palo Alto, CA, 2004) transformational leadership theory and discuss its relevance to cross-sector collaboration.

Keywords Network leader · Transformational leader · Idealized influence · Inspirational motivation · Individualized consideration

The degree to which leadership matters and is different in networks continues to be a debate among students and practitioners of public and nonprofit management. The style of leadership the network manager adopt is important as recent work has established that leadership has an effect on network performance (Jang et al. 2016; McGuire and Silvia 2009; Valero and Jang 2020; O'Leary et al. 2012). In this chapter, we explore the degree to which network managers exhibit leadership, the

H. S. Jang and J. N. Valero, *Public-Nonprofit Collaboration and Policy in Homeless Services*,
https://doi.org/10.1007/978-3-031-11918-7_4

leadership behaviors that matter most or are most used, and the effect that leadership has on network performance.

Based on their review of network research and years of consulting experience, Milward and Provan (2006) propose that effective collaboration requires network leaders to make critical decisions, manage the day-to-day affairs of the collaborative network, build trust, communicate network objectives to stakeholders, and hold other actors accountable for their roles and responsibilities. Thus, network leaders have an opportunity to place a focus on building positive social relations such as motivating and inspiring network members and ensuring that the individual needs of network members are carefully addressed. Network managers can adopt any number of leadership frameworks ranging from situational to style-based approaches. The literature in public administration has placed recent attention to the study of transformational leadership within public organizations (Belle 2014; Trottier et al. 2008) as well as in networks (Valero and Jang 2020). Transformational leadership style is seen in individuals that inspire and motivate followers toward a common vision, are open to new ideas, and place individual attention to the needs of followers (Bass and Avolio 1994). Given the hard work of addressing homelessness and the potential fragmentation across the sectors, transformational leadership can be a powerful explanatory variable in understanding effective management of homeless networks.

The application of transformational leadership to the context of interorganizational collaboration explains the dynamic interaction among network participants. This is because transformational leaders ultimately help create an environment of shared leadership by building relationships and a common vision. The collaboration process requires leaders that are stewards of the collaboration process, inspire others to work collaboratively by building consensus, consider the needs of network members and act as good faith mediators, and are open to new solutions and change when necessary (Ansell and Gash 2008; Chrislip and Larson 1994; Milward and Provan 2006).

According to Bass and Avolio (1994), transformational leaders can achieve these behaviors through its four dimensions: idealized influence, inspirational motivation, individualized consideration, and intellectual stimulation. *Idealized influence* refers to a leader who is a strong role model and whose behavior is led by strong ethical and moral standards. *Inspirational motivation* refers to leaders who motivate others by inspiring them to achieve mutual goals and who effectively link individual values and beliefs to the mission of the overarching organization. *Individualized consideration* refers to leaders who take an interest in the individual needs of others. Transformational leaders foster an environment of innovation and creativity through *intellectual stimulation*. In this type of environment, leaders and followers are able to exchange ideas, thoughts, and solutions to the ever-changing needs of an organization. In addition, this platform enables followers to challenge not only their values and beliefs, but also those of their leader and vice versa.

Although the transformational leadership instrument was originally developed for understanding leadership within single organizations, this leadership instrument offers solid model for effective management of public service networks such as CoCs. As such, this chapter modifies the original survey questions developed by Bass and Avolio (1994) to be in harmony with the context of networks.

A leader in public service collaboration has to maintain high ethical standards and be a strong role model in order for members of the network to accept network vision and goals through his or her idealized influence. Trottier et al. (2008), for example, investigate the perceived effectiveness of leadership style of employees who work in agencies within the executive branch in the United States and abroad. Their results indicate that federal employees perceive transformational leadership to be more effective than transactional leadership. Network leadership must motivate network members through inspiration to achieve common goals and objectives. Network leaders are expected, therefore, to also place value on the individual needs of stakeholders and accommodate those needs into decision-making processes. Lastly, network leaders exhibit intellectual stimulation by fostering an environment of shared leadership with other cross sector leaders and stakeholders of service community and creative exchange of ideas and approaches to serve clients with network members. In her study of nonprofit organizations focused on school dropout prevention services, for example, Jaskyte (2004) found that higher levels of transformational leadership explained technological and administrative innovation.

To understand leadership behaviors of CoC network leaders, we developed an online survey to the Collaborative Applicants or lead agency of 382 CoCs nationwide in 2016 (see Appendix 1 for survey questions). Modifying Bass and Avolio's transformational leadership to the network context, the survey was designed to learn more about how network leadership is carried out by Collaborative Applicants, to understand the collaboration (i.e., governance structure, communication strategies, and membership), and to investigate the degree to which network managers perceive that their networks are achieving successful outcomes. Transformational leadership was measured using 16 items and respondents were asked to answer each question using a five-point Likert-scale ranging from "never" to "very often." See Table 4.1 for list of measures for each dimension of transformational leadership. A total of 259 networks responded to your online national survey, for a response rate of about 68%. Our sample was reduced to 237 networks due to incomplete survey responses. Overall, 42 states were represented by our sample respondents.

Survey results indicate that network managers are placing a focus on respecting partner differences, instilling a fair process to their governance arrangement, and cultivating an environment of intellectual exchange. For instance, "seeking the counsel of key stakeholders of the network" (intellectual stimulation) was the most frequent transformational leadership behavior reported by CoC leaders. From this, we learn that the desired outcome of collaboration can be realized by gauging the interests and buy-in from key stakeholders. We also found that "being open to the ideas and suggestions of network members" (intellectual stimulation) was the second most frequent transformational leadership behavior reported, which confirms that network leaders make efforts to balance the collaboration's vision and participating organizations' mission and vision. The members of collaboration are likely to commit to network mission if their unique approaches to the collaborative goals are acknowledged and accepted. Thus, top two transformational leadership behaviors reported by network managers are part of the intellectual stimulation dimension.

The third most ranked leadership behavior—establishing a fair process in managing resources and inspiring a common vision—was part of the idealized influence dimension. This means that there is some level of recognition by network leaders that each organizational member differs, and as such, a relationship must be built by learning about the needs and interests of member agencies and ensuring that their requests are fairly considered in order to build a cohesive vision for the network.

The fourth ranked behavior—inspiring network members to work cohesively for common purpose—is a part of the inspirational motivation dimension of transformational leadership. This means that network leaders prioritize activities that help them build a collective vision for the network and securing support for this common purpose.

Table 4.1   Transformational leadership among CoC network managers

Dimension	Measure	Mean	Rank
Idealized influence	Considering the needs of network members before those of my own organization	4.0	6
	Instilling fairness in the process of managing resources in the network	4.2	3
	Expressing the need to adhere to ethical standards among members of the network	4.0	7
	Focusing efforts in building future leadership of network	3.3	16
Inspirational motivation	Inspiring network members to work cohesively for common purpose	4.1	4
	Expressing confidence in network members' ability to achieve network vision	3.9	8
	Making an effort to build a network vision to internal and external stakeholders of the network	3.8	10
	Helping each member of the network understand their unique role in network mission	3.6	13
Intellectual stimulation	Seeking the counsel of key stakeholders of the network	4.4	1
	Being open to the ideas and suggestions of network members	4.3	2
	Helping network members look at issues from different perspectives	4.0	5
	Creating opportunities for network members to engage in creativity and innovation	3.7	11
Individualized consideration	Providing assistance to network members so that they are able to overcome challenges they encounter	3.9	9
	Paying special attention to the individual needs and challenges of network members	3.7	12
	Teaching and coaching network members	3.6	14
	Helping assimilate new network members	3.6	15

Source Jang & Valero National CoC Leadership Survey 2016

In general, these results indicate that CoC network managers do indeed engage in leadership behaviors and that they, with great frequency, utilize transformational leadership. While intellectual stimulation was the highest rated dimension, it is clear that from observing the mean of each dimension, network managers see the benefit of engaging in varied aspects of transformational leadership.

Views on Leaders from the Frontlines[1]

To further understand the leadership of CoC network managers, we conducted a series of semi-structured interviews with CoC leaders in the summer of 2016 and asked them to describe their style of leadership in handling the affairs of their network. Cases for this study were selected from a sample of communities that had both responded to our national survey and functioned within communities with high incidences of homelessness. A general call for participation was sent to this sample and a total of 6 individuals responded positively. The interviews lasted about 1 hour and were focused on understanding the key network leadership behaviors that mattered most and why. Interview data was transcribed and coded for general themes.

Developing Subject Matter Expertise

Interviewees described the importance of being equipped with information, training, and best practices in homeless services in order to be an effective leader. Network managers are required to educate the public, to educate the public, political leaders, participating member agencies, and other service organizations, to lead conversations across the sectors to establish partnerships, and to secure necessary resources. This can be well done if fully informed and charged with data and know-how about the solutions necessary for making homelessness rare. For example, an interviewee in referring to their network leader described their leadership as follows:

[1] Earlier version of interview analysis was published at Jang, H., Valero, J., & Jung. K. 2016. "Effective Leadership in Network Collaboration: Lessons Learned from Continuum of Care Homeless Programs." IBM Center for the Business of Government (https://www.businessofgovernment.org/blog/effective-leadership-network-collaboration-lessons-learned-continuum-care-homeless-programs).

[Our network leader is] very knowledgeable about the demographics that we serve. I believe it is very important to be knowledgeable about service populations, so that you know what is going to take to actually end homelessness in your local community. She is also an expert in the field of homeless policies. She has been serving on several national committees on homelessness to be on track of what is going on in state and federal policies.

Nurture a Culture of Both Competition and Collaboration

While it may seem that competition and collaboration be at opposite ends of the spectrum on working together, interviews relate the value of instilling and nurturing a culture within the network that leads to both internal competition within the network and collaboration across the member organizations. For example, CoC networks compete on a yearly basis across the country for limited funding resources from the HUD. Interviewees noted that the national competition is so competitive, that is never for sure that every local proposal will be funded. So, to achieve innovation and generate the local proposals that might be most competitive at the national competition for funding, local networks suggest leading and establishing a local competitive process for being included in the CoC's final application for funding to HUD. The purpose is that local competition will generate novel ideas and solutions to ending homelessness.

At the same time, collaboration remains important for the continued work of the network. So many opportunities exist for cross-sector agencies to work together in dyads or larger to create programs or exchange information to help people step out of homelessness. One interviewee shared as follows:

During the NOFA[2] period, you ask them [member agencies] to compete against each other and talk about how better they are than the other agencies and the next month you ask them to play nice again as a team.

[2] NOFA refers to Notice of Funding Availability through which HUD announces that availability of funding for the next fiscal year.

Shared & Inclusive Leadership

Before the social justice movements of 2020, conversations about inclusivity and diversity were important and talked about in both the literature and practice. Particularly in the policy arena of homelessness, it is well understood that homelessness is a multidimensional problem and HUD encourages the participation of diversity of voices and stakeholders in the process—including the voice of formerly homeless individuals. Recent research has shown the impact that diversity can have in improved organizational performance (Harris 2014).

One network leader described the importance of being an inclusive leader. Her point is that "In this collaboration, every person that comes to a meeting is important." And it is only through the welcome environment the inclusive leader creates. Here is an example of being an inclusive leader and its benefit to the effective network.

> We have chronically homeless persons that regularly attend our general body meetings and they have a voice. Their input is very useful because sometimes we will be talking about something and they will shake their heads and say on the streets this is what it looks like. I didn't realize how big an impact that would have. What I love is the fact that they are welcomed like any other members of the community. I'm real proud of our general membership body because each of members are just like anybody else regardless if they are HUD funded or not.

Sharing responsibility and ownership of the joint work has also been regarded as an important tool for leading collaborations. In CoC networks, their governance structure begins with the creation of a governing board that is responsible for making decisions on behalf of the network. More advanced or mature networks, as our work has found, achieve governance in shared leadership models as well as through the creation of a network administrative organization (NAO). A significant proportion of the networks that responded to our national survey in 2016 informed that they have a governance structure that is shared among member agencies, and only a few networks establish a stand-alone 501(c)(3) public charity for CoC operations. From this finding, we learned that the daily management of the network will be left to the member organizations without designated personnel for the administration of grant applications and management of funding.

Thus, the inclusion of community stakeholders and affording them an opportunity to serve can help the network overcome challenges from lack of administrative capacity and help them advance its mission and vision. One network leader described benefits of having city official in their network. A recent study reported that CoC led by government agencies are more successful in acquisition of federal fundings compared to the networks led by nonprofit organizations (Valero et al. 2020). Their findings offers understanding about nonprofit organizational may face disadvantages in process of public grant proposal.

> We have a liaison from the city. She helps our agendas, and makes sure all of our network members get their email notifications. She also assists the Point-In-Time count data collection too. The city is really huge for our homeless network.

Be Agile

The policy and funding environment of homeless services is consistently changing, forcing networks to be in constant learning mode to adapt and overcome any possible disruptions. Through our case study work, we have learned of networks that have lost total funding, have merged with other networks to resolve service capacity, evolved into stand-alone nonprofits in the form of an NAO (Network Administrative Organization), created innovative partnerships to generate resources and exchange between community resource centers, and more. These have all been activities that have forced networks to adapt, to being agile, and achieve success. Thus, interviewees highlighted the importance of leadership that is responsive, adaptive, and simply agile to external and internal shocks to their local ecosystem.

For example, one of our interviewees was one of four members of a board leading the Cattaraugus County CoC in New York. In the most recent HUD funding cycle at the time of the study (2016), the network lost funding for its programs and the network board was left with a membership of two. This left the network leader to think carefully about the future of the network. She realized that the network could not be sustained and led by a single individual. As a result, the network is considering several options, one of which is to be merged with a neighboring network. Here, the network leader had accepted the reality of the network's evolution and was ready to adapt as necessary rather than staggering. In this process, it is also important not be afraid to ask for help especially when the network lacks administrative capacity. This is when having a strong local and national network of contacts is important to tap into for support and advice.

Be Smart with Data

CoC networks are expected to develop a Homeless Management Information System (HMIS) with the capacity to collect information on the extent and nature of homelessness, patterns of service use, and measurements of program effectiveness. Network leaders must realize the advantage in having access to data and information, and they must use them properly. Funding agencies, community stakeholders, and others come to expect data in order to understand the severity of a problem, allocate funding, and develop objective metrics of success in implementing local homeless programs. Securing new and unique data on the homeless population certainly creates an advantage. For instance, the Metro Dallas Homeless Alliance has developed a coordinated assessment tool and a comprehensive and up-to-date HMIS to track homeless services in the area. This allows the network to make a stronger case for why funding is needed and important for a new area of service.

REFERENCES

Ansell, Chris Ansell, and Alison Gash. 2008. Big Questions in Public Network Management Research. *Journal of Public Administration Research and Theory* 11 (3): 295–326.

Bass, Bernard M., and Bruce J. Avolio. 1994. *Improving Organizational Effectiveness Through Transformational Leadership*. Los Angeles, CA: Sage.

Bass, B.M., and B.J. Avolio. 2004. *Multifactor Leadership Questionnaire: Manual and Sample Set* 3rd ed. Palo Alto, CA: Mind Garden.

Bellé, Nicola. 2014. Leading to Make a Difference: A Field Experiment on the Performance Effects of Transformational Leadership, Perceived Social Impact, and Public Service Motivation. *Journal of Public Administration Research and Theory* 24 (1): 109–136.

Chrislip, David D., and Carl Larson. 1994. *Collaborative Leadership: How Citizens and Civic Leaders Can Make a Difference*. San Francisco: CA, Jossey-Bass.

Harris, E.E. 2014. The Impact of Board Diversity and Expertise on Nonprofit Performance. *Nonprofit Management and Leadership* 25: 113–130. https://doi.org/10.1002/nml.21115.

Jang, Hee Soun, Jesus N. Valero, and Kyujin Jung. 2016. *Effective Leadership in Network Collaboration: Lessons Learned from Continuum of Care Homeless Programs*. IBM Center for the Business Government.

Jaskyte, Kristina. 2004. Volunteer Involvement in Local Government After September 11: The Continuing Question of Capacity. *Public Administration Review* 65 (2): 131–142.

McGuire, M., and C. Silvia. 2009. Does leadership in networks matter? Examining the Effect of Leadership Behaviors on Managers' Perceptions of Network Effectiveness. *Public Performance & Management Review* 33, 34–62. https://doi.org/10.2753/PMR1530-9576330102 .

Milward, H. Brinton, and Keith G. Provan. 2006. *A Manager's Guide to Choosing and Using Collaborative Networks*. IBM Center for the Business Government.

O'Leary, Rosemary, Yujin Choi, and Catherine M. Gerard. 2012. The Skill Set of the Successful Collaborator. *Public Administration Review* 72 (s1): S70–S83.

Trottier, Tracey, Montgomery Van Wart, and XiaoHu Wang. 2008. Examining the Nature and Significance of Leadership in Government Organizations. *Public Administration Review* 68 (2): 319–333.

Valero, Jesus N., and Hee Soun Jang. 2020. The Effect of Transformational Leadership on Network Performance: A Study of Continuum of Care Homeless Networks. *Journal of Public and Nonprofit Affairs* 6 (3): 303–325.

Valero, Jesus N., D. Lee, and H. Jang. 2020. Public-Nonprofit Collaboration in Homeless Services: Are Nonprofit-Led Networks More Effective in Winning Federal Funding? *Administration and Society*. August.

CHAPTER 5

Cross-Sector Collaboration for Homeless Medical Services

Abstract Lack of access to the healthcare system is a significant factor leading to health inequities of people experiencing homelessness. In this chapter, We explore homeless medical services that require community collective responses and illustrate the challenges that CoC networks encounter in doing so in a collaborative manner. We report medical service demand of homeless population using national Point-In-Time (PIT) data and present federal and state laws related in service of homeless health care. From review of literature and consulting of service experts in medical field, 19 services are identified as healthcare services that are considered in demand for homeless individuals and families.

Keywords PATH grant · Emergency discharge coordination · Clinics in shelter · Mobile clinic

The needs of those experiencing homelessness are varied and complex, and chief among these needs is access to affordable healthcare services. The health inequity of homeless people has been reported that individuals experiencing homelessness are at higher risk of preventable diseases and also are less likely to access the healthcare system than most other populations. A study assessed unmet health needs of homeless population, and it reported that more than 70% of participating individuals experiencing homelessness have at least one unmet health issue, including medical and surgical care, medications, vision care, dental care, and mental health treatment (Baggett et al. 2010).

Lack of access to the healthcare system is a significant factor leading to health inequities (Baggett et al. 2010; Kertesz et al. 2009; Surber et al. 1988; Weitzman et al. 1996). Homeless people often delay treatment of medical conditions and leave health problems untreated until they reach a medical crisis and be admitted to an Emergency Department. Research reported that homeless veterans have greater medical and mental health needs and significantly less likely to access healthcare services. It is important to understand complex healthcare needs of those veterans who are homeless and their barriers in use of health care and engagement in medical treatment for a long-term care. The unmet healthcare needs of people experiencing homelessness make the services more expensive to treat. While homelessness as a policy issue that is touched by both federal and state/local laws, local entities such as nonprofits, local governments, and private hospitals bear significant responsibility in working directly with the homeless population, and in many situations, facilitating collaborative service integration to address the needs of individuals and families experiencing homelessness.

Medical service challenges to the communities require collective responses even when CoC networks focus on the housing-related demand of homeless individuals and families. Often systemic barriers are identified as factors challenging individuals and families to obtain proper medical care. The challenges tackling multidimensional medical and mental health problems are a substantial burden to community organizations, service providers, and advocates. CoC networks bear significant responsibility for coordinating efforts to address this important service need and the services the homeless demand are ranging from the struggle of shelter stability and food insecurity to mental and medical conditions and substance use problems. Among these needs, health care of homeless population is high in demand but low in response (Jang et al. 2020). This chapter places a focus on the medical service delivery functions of CoC networks, with special attention to the cross-sector collaboration to address the medical service needs of individuals experiencing homelessness, and presents type and variety of healthcare services made available across communities and the multidimensional factors that are associated with the extent to which communities are responding to the healthcare needs of a vulnerable population.

MEDICAL SERVICE NEEDS OF THE HOMELESS

The literature on the medical challenges and needs of the homeless is vast, with research documenting both the unique medical conditions and the factors contributing to these needs. However, less is known and understood about how local communities respond to the healthcare needs of the homeless through the CoCs' collaborative efforts. Because the needs of the homeless are complex and multidimensional, a collaborative service model is expected to effectively tackle the problem when service providers and others from the various sectors join forces. In addition, the CoC approach has been codified into law and federal resources have been invested with little knowledge of the degree to which this collaborative model is working to address the healthcare needs of a vulnerable population.

From the perspective of individuals experiencing homelessness, addressing their medical needs becomes a lower priority when challenged to meet very basic needs such as food and shelter (Committee on Community Health Services 1996). While there is a lack of national data documenting the specific medical needs of homeless individuals and families, HUD Point-In-Time data on homeless subpopulations sheds light on the characteristics of medical needs facing the homeless. Point-In-Time data is collected on a single night in January by CoC networks in an effort to count the number of homeless individuals in shelters and on the streets, and part of this effort involves documenting individuals facing medical challenges such as mental illness, substance use, and HIV/AIDS. As documented in Table 5.1, about 21% of the homeless population in the United States is severely mentally ill while 17% of the population faces a chronic substance abuse disorder. And about 2% of the U.S. homeless population has been diagnosed with HIV/AIDS and 8% report being victims of domestic violence. While these statistics do not directly identify the array of healthcare services that these individuals may need, the numbers certainly highlight the great potential for needed medical services. For example, homeless individuals with HIV/AIDS will require medication to control the virus and psychosocial treatment such as counseling and case management to cope with the idea of a life-threatening disease.

Table 5.1 Health service needs of the homeless, 2020

	Severally mentally Ill	Chronic substance abuse	HIV/AIDS	Victims of domestic violence	Unsheltered homeless population
National average	20.8%	17%	1.83%	8%	39%

Note Total homeless population was estimated at 580,466 from point-in-time count in 2020
Source 2020 HUD point-in-time report

Case studies of specific communities have also helped to document the unique medical challenges and needs of individuals experiencing homelessness. Acosta and Toro (2000), for example, similarly found that homeless adults in a community in New York State rate medical and dental care treatment as at least equally as important as housing. That same study of 301 homeless adults found, however, that homeless adults rate mental health and substance use services as relatively unimportant but easy to obtain or access. This is a striking finding when research also indicates that substance use, mental illness, and multi-morbidities are more common among homeless veteran groups than for housed veterans (Yuan et al. 2014), and homeless veterans experience higher all-cause mortality rates and rates of use of almost all resources (LePage et al. 2014). In another case study of neighborhood health centers in Los Angeles, a survey of homeless persons accessing services found that when compared to the poor who are housed, homeless individuals are more likely to have dermatological problems, functional limitations, chronic obstructive pulmonary disease, social isolation, serious vision problems, foot pain, and grossly decayed teeth (Gelberg et al. 1990).

Children experiencing homelessness also face necessary and often unmet healthcare needs. The Committee on Community Health Services notes that children face common acute problems such as respiratory tract infections, scabies, lice, rash, tooth decay, and ear infections (Weitzman et al. 1996). And when homeless children attend school, they are also more likely to have inconsistent attendance, grade repetition, and below-average performance (Committee on Community 1996). A study of a school-based mental and physical health prevention program and needs assessment found that homeless children access medical and dental care much less often than other children (Nabors et al. 2004). For example, only 17% of homeless children report seeing the same doctor on a regular or routine basis and report receiving fewer medical services, and more homeless youth report seeing a counselor when compared to other youth (Nabors et al. 2004).

FEDERAL LEGISLATION AND STATE LAW IN SERVICE OF HOMELESS HEALTH CARE

As noted in preceding sections, the HEARTH Act of 2009 and the CoC program specifically call attention to address the varied needs of the homeless, including healthcare needs. The membership composition of CoC networks must include medical sector entities such as hospitals, clinics, and substance use treatment centers and other health and human service nonprofits and community agencies.

State and local law varies from state to state, with some adopting more proactive policy and strategic plans to address the unique needs of their homeless population. For example, Texas created a program called Healthy Community Collaborative that authorized five cities to create a collaborative program (Senate Bill 58, 2013–2014). The funding and administrative support from this program are expected to promote collaboration among cross-sector service community for individuals with mental health issues and experiencing homelessness. In the State of California, the Department of Health Care Services (DHCS) manages the federally funded PATH (Projects for Assistance in Transition from Homelessness) grant program and distributes financial assistance to counties for their medical services and mental health programs for the homeless population. The distribution of the PATH program funding depends on the local needs and service demand of the local homeless population. Each county government under the PATH program is required to develop the strategic plans and budget annually for the services and programs, and their plan and budget should include services and programs for the homeless population served (more information about federal PATH grant program is provided in Fig. 5.1). Oregon state has established state law to respond to the medical service demand of homeless population and has been offering programs and services particularly targeted to individuals with mental illnesses experiencing homelessness (Oregon state law Chapter 430).[1]

---

[1] https://oregon.public.law/statutes/ors_chapter_430.

SAMHSA (Substance Abuse and Mental Health Services Administration) under federal Department of Health and Human Service manages Projects for Assistance in Transition from Homelessness (PATH), a formula based matching grant program which was established by the Stewart B. McKinney Homeless Assistance Amendments Act of 1990. PATH grant provides funding to all 50 states including U.S. territories and each state submit consolidated PATH proposals developed based on applications from local public and nonprofit PATH service providers. Even though the funding is a formula-based block grant, local providers may compete for funding award. Except U.S. territories, all states have to match one dollar to every three dollar federal funding.

According to SAMHSA websites there are about 500 PATH local service providers which offer services in support of mental health service programs. Here are services that can be funded by PATH grant.

- Outreach
- Screening and diagnostic treatment
- Habilitation and rehabilitation
- Community mental health
- Substance use disorders treatment
- Referrals for primary health care, job training, educational services, and housing
- Housing services as specified in Section 522(b)(10) of the Public Health Service Act

Fig. 5.1 Projects for assistance in transition from homelessness (PATH) grants (*Source* https://www.samhsa.gov/homelessness-programs-resources/grant-programs-services/path [Retrieved on May 29, 2022])

Homeless Emergency Discharge Coordination

When basic healthcare needs go unmet, homeless individuals are more likely to visit emergency rooms for nonemergency needs or for chronic health conditions. Homeless patients are commonly discharged to emergency shelters or the streets and those destinations will not have resources to support the healing process. When treated for acute medical needs, homeless individuals may need post-hospital care, but communities are challenged with lack of resources to provide adequate continuing health care and living arrangements that can help implement medical treatment (Gundlapalli et al. 2005). More resourced communities may offer medical respite care and other aftercare services to promote healing and to avoid high use of emergency rooms. Empirical evidence from a study done by Kertesz et al. (2009) found that post-hospital care is essential in order to implement medical recommendations and that when homeless people participate in a medical respite program, they are less likely to be readmitted within 90 days.

For an effective continuum of medical care for the homeless patients, the coordination of an emergency discharge plan is federally mandated policy (42 U.S. Code §11362, Discharge Coordination Policy) which demands local CoC to develop a coordination plan by engaging cross-sector and cross-service area actors and alleviating silos. However, this policy has been implemented as a recommendation to the CoCs as a checkbox in their HUD funding application rather than a required service capacity for funding eligibility. According to a CoC national survey conducted in 2018,[2] more than half (56%) of responding CoCs answered they do not have developed policies, plans, and/or protocols for individuals experiencing homelessness who have been discharged from healthcare institutions. Despite the benefits of an effective discharge plan, the coordination of commitment of diverse service providers demands leadership of CoC networks to initiate and connect stakeholders in housing, hospitals, healthcare providers, and cities and counties (Washington 2019). A case of CoC network #MN-503 (Dakota, Anoka, Washington, Scott, Carver Counties in Minnesota state)'s emergency discharge plan is presented in Fig. 5.2 as an example.

CoC Healthcare Service Capacities

In the spring of 2018, we launched a national survey of CoC networks with the specific goal of understanding the degree to which networks address the broad health and human service needs of their homeless population (see Jang et al. 2020). We identified a total of 356 CoC networks and collected 170 responses for a response rate of 48%.

The survey asked networks to identify the major health/medical services they provide the homeless and offers unique knowledge regarding the types and array of health services that local communities are providing for their homeless population. From review of literature and consulting of service experts in the medical field, 19 services were identified as health services that are considered in demand for homeless individuals and families. Table 5.2 provides details on the variety of healthcare services for the homeless and the extent to which CoCs provide each, and we list

[2] Jang & Valero (2018), Nation-wide survey titled, "A Study of Cross Sector Collaboration System for the Homeless".

MN-503 CoC: Dakota, Anoka, Washington, Scott, Carver Counties CoC

MN-503 Continuum of Care implements the discharge planning for foster care, health care, mental health, and corrections, consistent with Continuum of Care 101 (2009). For health care, there are many health services representing organizations as CoC network members such as local and community hospitals and health care providers in the specific areas. Committees in MN-503 and coordinated entry committee collaborate with community hospitals and develop the detailed plans of services and referral process for the individuals being discharged. Minnesota Statute requires counties to establish the discharge plans for all youth at 16 in foster care (Minn. Stat. ch. 245§ 4882, 2021).

CoC network continuously finds the places in the metro area for the housing and beds for the persons being discharged without stable housing. The people can stay until their medical treatments, or their health needs are finished or they can find permanent housing. Since 2011, the State of Minnesota has participated in the Money Follows the Person Rebalancing Demonstration which is a federal Medicaid program for long-term care services in the housing and plans to develop more available housing for the people being discharged in the medical needs.

Fig. 5.2   Emergency discharge coordination

them in ranking order from most to least. Table 2.1 offers the service frequency distribution of services provided by CoCs for understanding of varied health service capacity of local communities. One overall understanding from these analyses was that there are key health services that are mostly provided as basic health services for the homeless population. And about half of CoCs offer more than 50% of services from our list of key health services for the homeless. The results also indicate that most of local communities provide at least some type of healthcare service to the homeless, and beyond this, we found great variety in the number and type of services provided. The services that most CoCs tend to provide for homeless clients include: mental health care (95%), alcohol/substance use counseling (91%), supportive housing (87%), preventive services (82%), and wrap-around case management (80%).

The next grouping of healthcare services are provided by more than half of CoCs, and these services tend to be traditional medical services such as: prescription medicine (72%), dental care (68%), outreach clinic (56%), emergency care (52%), and medical or surgical care (52%).

Extant research has identified that clinics in shelter and mobile clinics are considered effective medial services that increase the homeless' access to the healthcare system and reduce preventable diseases that are often caused by infections, injuries, and acute conditions (Koh and O'Donnell 2016; Zlotnick et al. 2013; Christiani et al. 2008). Table 5.2 indicates

Table 5.2 Health services provided by CoCs for the homeless

Healthcare service	Percent of CoCs (%)
Mental healthcare	95
Alcohol/substance use counseling	91
Supportive housing	87
Preventive services	82
Wrap-around case management	80
Prescription medicine	72
Dental care	68
Outreach clinic	56
Emergency care	52
Medical or surgical care	52
Eye glasses	47
Clinic in shelter	47
Mobile clinic	47
Methadone clinics	33
Syringe exchange	26
Suboxone clinic	26
Assisted living	22
Nursing beds at shelter	20
Hospice care	18

Source Valero & Jang National CoC Survey 2018

that little less than half (47%) of CoCs that responded to our survey is providing clinics in shelters and mobile clinic services to their homeless population. The clinics in shelter and mobile clinics will have the physicians and nurses who will bring direct medical services to the streets and shelters where the homeless are. It is our expectation that these services will offer homeless patients more consistent and continuous primary care and will be a better approach of caring for individuals in a cost-effective way.

Specialized and proactive medical response to substance abuse was provided less as a provided healthcare service by local communities. For example, 33% of CoCs provide methadone clinics, 26% have a syringe exchange program, and 26% have a suboxone clinic in their community.

Lastly, results show that the lowest among services provided are the more substantial service arrangements for long-term medical care of the homeless patients. Research on health care for homeless population indicates the critical value and high demand of medical respite services for the continuity of care for improving medical conditions of homeless

Table 5.3 Frequency distribution of medical service provision by CoCs

Number health services provided	Number of CoCs
19–15 services	22 (13%)
14–10 services	78 (46%)
9–6 services	51 (30%)
5 and less services	19 (11%)

This table was a part of authors' published article, Jang et al. (2020), "A Study of Cross-Sector Health Care Services for the Homeless: Community Health Service Capacity Measured and Tested." *Journal of Health and Human Services Administration.* Vol. 42 (2). P. 187.

patients (Koh and O'Donnell 2016). While these may save costs in the long run, the initial investment required may be difficult to overcome for many communities. CoCs, for instance, report the following services: 22% assisted living services, 20% have nursing beds at the shelter, and 18% provide hospice care.

Table 5.3 captures the frequency distribution of medical service provision for the homeless across the nation from survey respondents. Results indicate that 13% or 22 CoCs provide 15 to 19 healthcare services to the homeless. For example, homeless service communities of Tucson/Pima county (AZ) and Boston (MA) provide most of the services we listed in our survey.[3] The largest proportion of CoCs tend to provide 10–14 different healthcare services. About 30% of CoCs or 51 total provide 6–9 services to individuals experiencing homeless. We found 19 CoCs (11%) provide 5 or less healthcare services from our list of healthcare questions. It was notable that among 22 CoCs in our top category, we found 17 CoCs responded that they have a subcommittee or a work group that coordinates medical and health services for homeless population in their CoC network. Contrary to this group, none of CoCs that provide 5 services or less reported that they have subgroup focus on medical and health services.

[3] CoCs provide most of the services (19–17 services) we listed in our survey are: Tucson/Pima county (AZ), Boston (MA), San Francisco (CA), Richmond/Contra Costa (CA), Miami Dade county (FL), Las Vergas/Clark county (NV), Long Beach (CA), and Pittsburgh, McKeesport, Penn Hills/Allegheny county (PA).

REFERENCES

Acosta, Olan, and Paul A. Toro. 2000. Let's Ask the Homeless People Themselves: A Needs Assessment Based on a Probability Sample of Adults. *American Journal of Community Psychology* 28 (3): 343–366.

Baggett, T.P., J.J. O'Connell, D.E. Singer, and N.A. Rigotti. 2010. The Unmet Health Care Needs of Homeless Adults: A National Study. *American Journal of Public Health* 100 (7): 1326–1333.

Christiani, A., A.L. Hudson, A. Nyamathis, M. Mutere, and J. Sweat. 2008. Attitudes of Homeless and Drug-Using Youth Regarding Barriers and Facilitators in Delivery of Quality and Culturally Sensitive Health Care. *Journal of Child and Adolescent Psychiatric Nursing* 21 (3): 154–163.

Committee on Community Health Services. 1996. Health Needs of Homeless Children and Families. *Pediatrics* 98 (4): 789–791.

Discharge Coordination Policy, 42 U.S.C. §11362. 2011.

Gelberg, Lillian, Lawrence S. Linn, Richard P. Usatine, and Mary H. Smith. 1990. Health, Homelessness, and Poverty: A Study of Clinic Users. *Archives of Internal Medicine* 150 (11): 2325–2330.

Gundlapalli, Adi, Monte Hanks, Scott M. Stevens, Amy M. Geroso, Christopher R. Viavant, Yvonne McCall, Patrick Lang, Michael Bovos, Nicholas T. Branscomb, and Allan D. Ainsworth. 2005. It Takes a Village: A Multidisciplinary Model for the Acute Illness Aftercare of Individuals Experiencing Homelessness. *Journal of Health Care for the Poor and Underserved* 16 (2): 257–272.

Jang, H., J.N. Valero, and J. Jeong. 2020. A Study of Cross-Sector Health Care Services for the Homeless. Community Health Service Capacity Measured and Tested. *Journal of Health and Human Services Administration* 43 (2): 178–195.

Kertesz, Stefan G., Michael A. Posner, James J. O'Connell, Stacy Swain, Ashley N. Mullins, Shwartz Michael, and Arlene S. Ash. 2009. Post-Hospital Medical Respite Care and Hospital Readmission of Homeless Persons. *Journal of Prevention & Intervention in the Community* 37 (2): 129–142.

Koh, Howard K., and James J. O'Connell. 2016. Improving Health Care for Homeless People. *JAMA* 316 (24): 2586–2587.

LePage, James P., D.J. Ledjona Bradshaw, and D.J. Cipher, and A.M. Crawford. 2014. The Effects of Homelessness on Veterans' Health Care Service Use: An Evaluation of Independence from Comorbidities. *Public Health* 128 (11): 985–992.

Nabors, Laura A., Mark D. Weist, Ryan Shugarman, Michael J. Woeste, Elizabeth Mullet, and Leah Rosner. 2004. Assessment, Prevention, and Intervention Activities in a School-Based Program for Children Experiencing Homelessness. *Behavior Modification* 28 (4): 565–578.

Senate Bill 58. 2013–2014. Relating to Delivery of and Reporting on Mental Health, Behavioral Health, Substance Abuse, and Certain other Services. Texas Senate Bill 58, 83rd legislature Texas-2013-SB58-Enrolled (legiscan.com).

Surber, Robert W., Eleanor Dwyer, Katherine J. Ryan, Stephen M. Goldfinger, and John T. Kelly. 1988. Medical and Psychiatric Needs of the Homeless—A Preliminary Response. *Social Work* 33 (2): 116–119.

The Homeless Emergency Assistance and Rapid Transition to Housing Act 2009 (HEARTH). S. 896 (US).

Washington, Federickia L. 2019. Study of Homeless Emergency Discharge Coordination: Understanding Challenges and Success Factors to Collaboration Maturity (Doctoral Dissertation, University of North Texas) (Open Access Dissertation) https://digital.library.unt.edu/ark:/67531/metadc1609098/.

Weitzman, S., Fisch, Jr. Holmberg, R.E. Jackson, A.D. Lisbin, C.J. McKay, P. Melinkovich, R.L. Meuli, Y.L. Piovanetti, A.E. Dyson, L.K. Grossman, J.A. McLaurin, C. Poland, J.S. Schultz, M.S. Jones, and D. O'Hare. 1996. Health Needs of Homeless Children and Families. *PEDIATRICS* 98 (4): 789–791.

Yuan, Sarah, Hong Vo, and Kristen D. Gleason. *Homeless Service Utilization Report: Hawai'i 2014*. Honolulu, HI: University of Hawai'i Center on the Family.

Zlotnick, Cheryl, Suzanne Zerger, and Phyllis B. Wolfe. 2013. Health Care for the Homeless: What We Have Learned in the Past 30 Years and What's Next. *American Journal of Public Health* 103 (Suppl2): 199–205.

CHAPTER 6

Measuring Effective Collaboration and the Factors that Matter

Abstract Measuring collaboration performance is a challenge for communities when no one community is the same and the incidence of homelessness is varied. We offer a review of literature on ways to understand and measure performance of CoC networks and the degree to which they are effective collaborative arrangements. This chapter presents a CoC network effectiveness model by considering the degree to which organizations achieve success at both the network and community level using Provan and Milward's (2001) framework for evaluating public sector networks as a lens. In this chapter, we discuss four major conditions that will be important to consider for effective performance of homeless service networks: (1) nonprofit-led public service networks, (2) network leading experience, (3) network membership, and (4) effective leadership styles.

Keywords Network effectiveness · Network level measure · Organizational level measures · Community level measures · Network activation

The underlying assumption in the adoption of the Continuum of Care (CoC) approach as the method to reduce and eliminate homelessness

H. S. Jang and J. N. Valero, *Public-Nonprofit Collaboration and Policy in Homeless Services*,
https://doi.org/10.1007/978-3-031-11918-7_6

is that collaboration is the most effective way of tackling this wicked problem. Thus, the study of collaboration in public and nonprofit management is increasingly an area of interest sparked by its purported existence in practice and movements to reinvent public services—among other factors. However, the least attention has been paid to the study of collaboration processes or the "doing" of collaboration and to understanding outcomes of collaboration. This is not surprising when it is difficult to observe the complex interaction of cross-sector actors participating in the multi-stages of the collaboration process and it is even more challenging to identify collective goals shared among members of collaboration and their corresponding measurable collaboration outcomes.

Despite the prevalence of CoC homeless networks across the United States and the nearly 2.2 billion dollars in HUD competitive funding awarded to these networks in 2020, there has been little research conducted to assess the degree to which cross-sector organizations within CoCs are effective in achieving mutual goals and objectives (HUD Exchange 2022).[1] This chapter discusses diverse ways to understand and measure performance of public service networks and the degree to which they are effective collaborative arrangements. Measuring effective collaboration is a challenge for communities when no one community is the same and the incidence of homelessness is varied. This chapter focuses on answering the following questions: In what ways can effective collaboration be conceptualized for homeless serving CoC networks? What factors are associated with differences in collaboration effectiveness across CoC networks?

This chapter presents a CoC network effectiveness model by considering the degree to which organizations achieve success at both the network and community levels using Provan and Milward's (2001) framework for evaluating public sector networks as a lens. This chapter examines ways of measuring CoC collaboration effectiveness at various levels and presents the key factors that matter in effective collaboration.

---

[1] https://www.hudexchange.info/news/hud-awards-nearly-2-2-billion-to-local-homeless-programs/ (retrieved May 19, 2022).

Effective Collaboration in Social Services

The management of collaboration is different from management of single organization, and the challenges of collaboration may demand unique sector leadership, network capacities to the governance, and leadership to address management difficulties of collaboration. Collaboration literature helps us understand key factors that may affect effective collaboration for services for the homeless and how these conditions result in positive collaboration outcomes.

Effective collaboration—broadly defined—refers to the degree to which organizations in collaboration are able to achieve successful outcomes (Gazley 2010; Selden et al. 2006). To date, most of the collaboration effectiveness research has focused on understanding conditions or factors that may help organizations accumulate individual benefits through the collaboration process such as improved client outcomes and access to additional resources (Andrews and Entwistle 2010; Babiak 2009; Chen and Graddy 2010; Gazley 2010; Gazley and Brudney 2007; Provan and Milward 1995; Selden et al. 2006).

In a seminal piece on assessing network effectiveness, Provan and Milward (2001) suggested that network effectiveness research could be conducted at three levels of analysis: organization, network, and community. We adopt Provan and Milward's model of network effectiveness in this chapter. At the *organization level*, the focus is on assessing the degree to which organizations are able to accumulate individual benefits as a result of their collaborative participation. For example: Are organizations able to better serve their client base as a result of collaborating with other organizations? An organization may be able to improve its client services by accessing resources and information that may help it better understand and serve the needs of its clients. At the *network level*, effectiveness is measured by considering the degree to which the network as a whole is able to achieve collective benefits such as increased membership, resource accquisition, and building network legitimacy and advocacy of the network cause. Here, the interest is not on individual benefits but on the extent to which the network, as a whole body, achieves outcomes that benefit everyone. By increasing membership, for example, the network is able to better serve the multidimensional needs of homeless people within its community. At the *community level*, the focus is on assessing whether the network is able to contribute value to the community it serves such as a reduction in the problem the network is addressing. In the case of homeless networks, are these networks reducing the incidence of homelessness? After all, the chief purpose of homeless network is to address the homelessness rate within their community. Table 6.1 presents three levels of network effectiveness and suggested measures for each level at the CoC homeless service context.

Andrews and Entwistle (2010), for example, explore the impact of different types of cross-sectoral partnership arrangements on collaboration effectiveness. Effectiveness in that study was measured at the organizational level by investigating the degree to which clients completed an educational program. Their study found that public-public partnerships matter in explaining an increase in effectiveness, but public-nonprofit partnerships do not result in statistically significant results. These results indicate that organizations must be aware of the costs and benefits that different types of partnership arrangements may have on collaboration outcomes.

Table 6.1 Network effectiveness measures

CoC Network Effectiveness	Concepts	Suggested measures
Organization level	• Are organizations able to better serve their client base as a result of collaborating with other organizations?	• Client references • Participating in consolidated grant proposals • Service data shared • New resources acquired
Network level	• What is the degree to which the network as a whole is able to achieve collective benefits?	• HUD funding secured and increased • Designated as High Performing Community (HPC) from HUD • New member agencies participated • New service contract developed • Advocacy action made
Community level	• Does the network contribute value to the community it serves?	• Reduction of homelessness • Reduction of unsheltered homeless • Permanent supportive housing increased

In a study of social service networks, collaboration effectiveness was measured at the organizational level by using subjective and organizational level measures such as client goal achievement and improved organizational learning (Chen and Graddy 2010). Some research has explored network effectiveness at the network level, but those studies also use subjective measures of effectiveness and adopt case study or qualitative approaches (Babiak and Thibault 2009; Chen 2008; Nolte and Boenigk 2013). In a case study of family and children services in Los Angeles county, for instance, Chen (2008) analyzes the impact of collaboration processes on perceived network level effectiveness measures such as the quality of working relationships, increasing partner interactions, and goal achievement. The collaboration processes that Chen (2008) considered included: joint decision-making, joint operation, reduced organizational autonomy, resource sharing, and building trust. In general, the results of their study found that resource sharing and building trust mattered in explaining perceived collaboration outcomes.

Studies on community level effectiveness are rare. In a case study of three multi-sectoral workforce development networks, Herranz (2010) finds that some network coordination strategies matter more in explaining community level performance such as job placement rate and service integration. The limitation of that study is that it was unable to establish any causal relationships and instead, provided an initial exploration of Provan and Milward's (2001) theoretical framework.

Extant scholarship has focused on assessing the external conditions of a network that foster effective collaborations; little, however, is known about the key conditions that affect the effective management of multi-layered, collaborative networks. In this chapter, we discuss four major conditions that will be important to consider for effective performance of homeless service networks: (1) nonprofit leadership in public service networks, (2) network leading experience, (3) network membership, and (4) effective leadership styles.

FACTORS INFLUENCING EFFECTIVE COLLABORATION

Nonprofit Leadership in Public Service Networks

Nonprofit organizations have been considered well-positioned in service delivery in partnership with government as suggested by Salamon's Third Party Government Theory (1987), which posits that nonprofits are better equipped to deliver social services because they are community based, have more knowledge and experience and closer to the clients, and not bound by rigid bureaucratic restrictions compared to government agencies. As Dennis Young (1998) notes, there is a comparative advantage to the nonprofit organizations in their service delivery role when we assess the benefits nonprofits will bring in to the public service. The focus of these theories invoke a notion that nonprofits are more efficient in the delivery of services whereas government is better at creating policy and funding public programs. However, on the other side of coin, these advantages of nonprofit organizations being community based and helping their local community make them have trust-based relationships with other community organizations and achieve acknowledgment among key stakeholders of the service area (Ott and Dicke 2012; Schneider 2009; Wolf 1999). This community legitimacy and trust place nonprofits in an advantageous position of even leading the activation process of the public service collaboration.

Several scholars have noted that activation of network is a crucial initial step in the collaboration formation process where a lead organization, such as a human service nonprofit, identifies potential members of a network in the community, invites key stakeholders, and actively coordinates engagement of diverse members and manages solid membership of participants. A study done by Johnston and his colleagues (2011) reports that achieving broad inclusion of stakeholders in the collaborative process "is an important but often overlooked aspect of implementation" (p. 699). Nonprofit organizations when they lead the network can achieve this broad inclusion of stakeholders by tapping into their existing organizational social capital in the community (Schneider 2009). In their 10-year study of partnerships between public and community-based nonprofits, Alexander and Nank (2009) also find that community-based nonprofit organizations often function as a bridge between the community and government agencies.

Successful leadership in the public service collaboration has to engage in selling a mission and vision to potential partners and other stakeholders and provide a clear direction and purpose to the network members (Milward and Provan 2006; Silvia 2011). Nonprofits tend to be well connected to the community they serve and to have established relationships with community leaders, which translate into established trust with third parties. For example, in their study of British nonprofit organizations, Eng et al. (2012) found that the charitable and social mission nature of nonprofits help enhance trustworthiness in relationally embedded network ties and that nonprofits tend to leverage on their social mission to improve their ability to secure resources.

Network Leading Experience

Realizing that network management is no easy task and often different from managing a single organization (Silvia and McGuire 2010; Valero and Jang 2016), the network management experience accumulated over time will matter in explaining more favorable network performance. Previous case study work on network governance has found that a lack of proper skills or experience can be detrimental to the collaborative process (Cornforth et al. 2015), and in our research (Valero, Lee and Jang 2020), we systematically test whether this idea holds true. Moreover, securing federal grants can be a complex and cumbersome process, but with time, comes experience in navigating the grants process. Thus, leading agencies who have more experience managing and leading the collaboration process may accumulate knowledge that may prove valuable in securing network resources.

The scholarship on collaborative governance suggests that those in charge of leading a collaborative service network exercise a variety of management activities ranging from maintaining stable memberships, holding partner agencies accountable to identifying and securing resources (Milward and Provan 2006). Leaders of networks have to manage resource identification, maintenance, and development, and these resource managing tasks are important step especially in the initial stage of a collaboration (Agranoff and McGuire 2001; Fountain 2013; McGuire 2002). And certainly, the failure to secure necessary resources and maintain an effective governance process can impact the performance and survivability of the network (Cornforth et al. 2015). In their survey of county emergency managers, for example, McGuire and Silvia (2009) find that network managers rate the "identifying resources" as a top network activation and leadership behavior. In another study on homeless collaboration, Jang and her colleagues (2016), in their national study of homeless service, also find that network managers rate identifying resources as a top responsibility of leading their networks.

Membership of Network Collaboration

In their meta-analytical study of existing research on collaborative governance, Ansell and Gash (2008) propose that identifying potential members and establishing ground rules for the members are other important network design factors that impact the collaboration process and collective goal achievement. And some research conceptualizes the size of membership as a measure of the capacity of network collaboration (LeRoux et al. 2010; MacIndoe 2013). Empirically, other research verifies the size of membership as a significant factor to improve collaborative performances. Yi (2018) finds that the network size, which is measured by the number of membership in the local energy policy network, brings increases in renewable energy capacity. In their study of social service networks, Marrio and Cristofoli (2017) find the network endurance, measured by the range and quality of services provided by network, is positively affected by the size of partner organizations in social service networks. The engagement of a large number of participants in the network is a way of measuring intensity of collaborative interactions and we observe it by counting the number of member agencies within service networks. The ability of engaging a number of members and maintaining these members in the network arrangement is a key and necessary condition for the effective management of public service networks and ultimately generate positive network performance.

The literature is far from conclusive on the optimum number of actors that should be involved in the collaboration process. While there is no precise number of organizations or members that should partake in the collaborative process, a large membership size of network is a proxy or sign of a network that is more inclusive of the community and of stakeholders. In preparing a grant application for funding from the federal government, inclusivity may pay dividends for networks in numerous ways, including sending a strong message of support from the community about the value and need of the proposed projects as well as leveraging the resources and capacity of more members of the community in actually producing the application.

Role of Leadership in Collaboration

The style of leadership that a network leader exhibits matters in collaboration outcomes. Gazley (2010), for example, calls "for a more nuanced look at the characteristics of the public managers who make collaborative decisions" (669). Milward and Provan (2006) propose that effective collaboration requires effective network management including holding members accountable, maintaining communication, and building cohesive strategies. These network leader responsibilities can be categorized as either task behaviors or relationship behaviors, which Northouse (2010) suggests comprise the style approach of leadership. Task behaviors are focused on facilitating network goal achievement, such as identifying roles and responsibilities, holding network members accountable for performance, and putting plans into action. Relationship behaviors, on the other hand, place a greater focus on building positive social relations such as motivating and inspiring network members and ensuring that the individual needs of members are carefully addressed.

Two leadership theories show why the task and relationship behaviors on collaborative outcomes matter: collaboration leadership theory (Agranoff and McGuire 2001; McGuire 2002; McGuire and Silvia 2009) and transformational leadership theory (Bass and Avolio 1994). These two leadership styles have been posited as explanations for leadership activities that facilitate effective collaboration among organizations. Collaboration leadership theory provides a foundation for the task behaviors that are necessary for network leaders to perform and transformational leadership speaks to the relationship behaviors that are important for building relationships, commitment, and social capital. Although they are different styles of leadership, both are likely to overlap. Both styles of leadership can be understood as important behaviors that are necessary for managing the different aspects of a collaborative network. Higher levels of transformational and collaborative leadership, for example, are likely to result in higher levels of collaborative effectiveness (see Fig. 6.1).

McGuire and Silvia (2009) propose that collaborative leadership is comprised of four task behaviors and test the extent to which these matter in perceived network effectiveness among county emergency managers. *Activation* refers to the process by which the leader identifies key members of the network, while *mobilization* is concerned with building the support of important stakeholders both internal and external. *Framing* refers to the process by which the leader identifies the mission and vision of the network. *Synthesizing* behaviors are focused on building consensus among network members and fostering an environment that results in productive interactions.

	Low Collaborative Leadership	High Collaborative Leadership
Low Transformational Leadership	**Low Effectiveness**	**Moderate Effectiveness**
High Transformational Leadership	**Moderate Effectiveness**	**High Effectiveness**

Fig. 6.1 Leadership in effective collaboration

Whereas collaborative leadership theory is predominantly concerned with task behaviors, leaders in collaboration setting have to present relationship behaviors and concerns and we use transformational leadership theory that places a greater focus on relationship behaviors in understanding leadership factors in effective collaborations. As noted earlier in Chapter 4, transformational leadership is observed through idealized influence, inspirational motivation, individualized consideration, and intellectual stimulation—all behaviors that point to a leader that is attentive to individual needs, can connect individual interests to the collective interests, isn't afraid of hearing diverse opinions, and inspires members to work together.

As noted in Fig. 5.2, our research has found that both styles of leadership matter (Jang et al. 2016). And that when CoC homeless network managers exhibit both styles interchangeably based on the situation at hand, they may be more effective in achieving network outcomes. When one style is used more than the other, the resulting impact is moderate. When neither is used, network managers will achieve low network impact.

REFERENCES

Agranoff, Robert, and Michael McGuire. 2001. Big Questions in Public Network Management Research. *Journal of Public Administration Research and Theory* 11 (3): 295–326.

Alexander, Jennifer, and Renee Nank. 2009. Public—Nonprofit Partnership: Realizing the New Public Service. *Administration & Society* 41 (3): 364–386.

Andrews, Rhys, and Tom Entwistle. 2010. Does Cross-Sectoral Partnership Deliver? An Empirical Exploration of Public Service Effectiveness, Efficiency, and Equity. *Journal of Public Administration Research and Theory* 20 (3): 679–701.

Ansell, Chris, and Alison Gash. 2008. Collaborative Governance in Theory and Practice. *Journal of Public Administration Research & Theory* 18 (4): 543–571.

Babiak, Kathy M. 2009. Criteria of Effectiveness in Multiple Cross-Sectoral Interorganizational Relationships. *Evaluation and Program Planning* 32 (1), 1–12 (ISSN 0149-7189). https://doi.org/10.1016/j.evalprogplan.2008.09.004.

Babiak, Kathy, and Lucie Thibault. 2009. Challenges in Multiple Cross-Sector Partnerships. *Nonprofit and Voluntary Sector Quarterly* 38 (1): 117–143. https://doi.org/10.1177/0899764008316054.

Bass, Bernard M, and Bruce J Avolio. 1994. *Improving organizational effectiveness through transformational leadership*. Sage Publication, Inc.

Chen, Bin. 2008. Assessing Interorganizational Networks for Public Service Delivery: A Process-Perceived Effectiveness Framework. *Public Performance & Management Review* 31 (3): 348–363.

Chen, Bin, and Elizabeth A. Graddy. 2010. The effectiveness of nonprofit lead-organization networks for social service delivery. *Nonprofit Management & Leadership* 20 (4): 405–422.

Cornforth, Chris, John Paul Hayes, and Siv Vangen. 2015. Nonprofit–Public Collaborations: Understanding Governance Dynamics. *Nonprofit and Voluntary Sector Quarterly* 44 (4): 775–795.

Eng, Teck-Yong., Chih-Yao Gordon. Liu, and Yasmin Kaur Sekhon. 2012. The Role of Relationally Embedded Network Ties in Resource Acquisition of British Nonprofit Organizations. *Nonprofit and Voluntary Sector Quarterly* 41 (6): 1092–1115.

Fountain Jane E. 2013. *Implementing Cross-Agency Collaboration a Guide for Federal Managers Collaborating Across Boundaries Series*. IBM Center for the Business Government.

Gazley, Beth. 2010. Linking Collaborative Capacity to Performance Measurement in Government-Nonprofit Partnerships. *Nonprofit and Voluntary Sector Quarterly* 39 (4): 653–673.

Gazley, B., and J.L. Brudney. 2007. The Purpose (and Perils) of Government–Nonprofit Partnership. *Nonprofit and Voluntary Sector Quarterly* 36, 389–415. https://doi.org/10.1177/0899764006295997.

Herranz, Jr.J. 2010. Multilevel Performance Indicators for Multisectoral Networks and Management. *The American Review of Public Administration* 40 (4): 445–460. https://doi.org/10.1177/0275074009341662

HUD Exchange. 2022. https://www.hudexchange.info/. Retrieved June 1, 2022.

Jang, Hee Soun, Jesus N. Valero, and Kyujin Jung. 2016. *Effective Leadership in Network Collaboration: Lessons Learned from Continuum of Care Homeless Programs.* IBM Center for the Business Government.

Johnston, Erik W., Darrin Hicks, Ning Nan, and Jennifer C. Auer. 2011. Managing the Inclusion Process in Collaborative Governance. *Journal of Public Administration Research and Theory* 21 (4): 699–721.

LeRoux, K., P.W. Brandenburger, and S.K. Pandey. 2010. Interlocal Service Cooperation in US Cities: A Social Network Explanation. *Public Administration Review* 70, 268–278. https://doi.org/10.1111/j.1540-6210.2010.02133.x.

MacIndoe, H. 2013. Reinforcing the Safety Net: Explaining the Propensity for and Intensity of Nonprofit–Local Government Collaboration. *State and Local Government Review* 45 (4): 283–295. https://doi.org/10.1177/0160323X13515004.

Marrio, and Cristofoli. 2017. How to Support the Endurance of Long-Term Networks: The Pivotal Role of the Network Manager. *Public Administration* 95 (4): 1060–1075.

McGuire, Michael. 2002. Managing Networks: Propositions on What Managers Do and Why They Do It. *Public Administration Review* 62 (5): 599–609.

McGuire, Michael, and Chris Silvia. 2009. Does Leadership in Networks Matter? Examining the Effect of Leadership Behaviors on Managers' Perceptions of Network Effectiveness. *Public Performance and Management Review* 33 (1): 34–62.

Milward, H. Brinton, and Keith G. Provan. 2006. *A Manager's Guide to Choosing and Using Collaborative Networks.* IBM Center for the Business Government.

Nolte, Isabella M., and Silke Boenigk. 2013. A Study of Ad Hoc Network Performance in Disaster Response. *Nonprofit and Voluntary Sector Quarterly* 42 (1): 148–173.

Northouse, Peter Guy. 2010. Leadership: Theory and Practice/Peter G. Northouse.-5th ed. p. cm.

Ott, Steve, and Lisa A. Dicke. 2012. *The Nature of the Nonprofit Sector.* Philadelphia, PA: Westview Press.

Provan, Keith G., and H. Brinton Milward. 1995. A Preliminary Theory of Interorganizational Network Effectiveness: A Comparative Study of Four

Community Mental Health Systems. *Administrative Science Quarterly* 40 (1): 1–33.

Provan, Keith G., and H. Brinton Milward. 2001. Do Networks Really Work? A Framework for Evaluating Public-Sector Organizational Networks. *Public Administration Review* 61 (4): 414–423.

Salamon, Lester M. 1987. Of Market Failure, Voluntary Failure, and Third-Party Government: Toward a Theory of Government-Nonprofit Relations in the Modern Welfare State. *Nonprofit and Voluntary Sector Quarterly* 16 (1–2): 29–49.

Schneider, Jo Anne. (2009). Organizational Social Capital and Nonprofits. *Nonprofit and Voluntary Sector Quarterly* 38 (4): 643–662.

Selden, Sally Coleman, Jessica E. Sowa, and Jodi Sandfort. 2006. The Impact of Nonprofit Collaboration in Early Child Care and Education on Management and Program Outcomes. *Public Administration Review* 66 (3): 412–425.

Silvia, Chris. 2011. Collaborative Governance Concepts for Successful Network Leadership. *State and Local Government Review* 43 (1): 66–71.

Silvia, Chris, and Michael McGuire. 2010. Leading Public Sector Networks: An Empirical Examination of Integrative Leadership Behaviors. *The Leadership Quarterly* 21 (2): 264–277.

Valero, Jesus N., and Hee Soun Jang. 2016. The Role of Nonprofit Organizations in Homeless Policy Networks. *Cityscape: A Journal of Policy Development and Research* 18 (2): 151–162.

Valero, J.N, D. Lee, and H. Jang. 2020. Public-Nonprofit Collaboration in Homeless Services: Are Nonprofit-Led Networks More Effective in Winning Federal Funding? *Administration and Society* (August).

Wolf, Thomas. 1999. *Managing a Nonprofit Organization: Updated Twenty-First-Century Edition*. New York, NY: Free Press.

Yi, Hongtao. 2018. Network Structure and Governance Performance: What Makes a Difference? *Public Administration Review* 78 (2): 195–205.

Young, Dennis R. 1998. Commercialism in Nonprofit Social Service Associations: Its Character, Significance, and Rationale. *Journal of Public Analysis and Management* 17 (2): 278–297.

CHAPTER 7

Conclusion

Abstract This chapter discusses the contributions of this work to the theory and practice of public policy, collaborative governance and role of nonprofit organizations in cross-sector collaboration. For students and teachers in the fields of public administration, policy, and nonprofit management, we present ways that this book contributes to existing knowledge base and directions for future research. We offer policy and management recommendations for those engaged in homeless service collaboration through CoC networks and provide key lessons that organizations participating in public service networks can employ to manage and lead collaborations.

Keywords Multi-sector actors · Access to healthcare system · Best practices · Strategies · Management skills

We began this book on to take a deeper look into the work and efforts of a novel collaborative mechanism, namely Continuum of Care homeless networks in the United States. Collaborative governance has become a dominant form of governance, and the CoC networks attempt to achieve collaborative governance for the purpose of reducing the incidence of homelessness across the U.S. communities. Collaborative governance is

© The Author(s), under exclusive license to Springer Nature
Switzerland AG 2023
H. S. Jang and J. N. Valero, *Public-Nonprofit Collaboration
and Policy in Homeless Services*,
https://doi.org/10.1007/978-3-031-11918-7_7

accepted as the key strategy by both HUD and the U.S. Interagency Council on Homelessness because it has power to pool fragmented community service providers and resources of all kinds in order to better support and streamline services for people experiencing homelessness.

While collaboration across the sectors has become a common governance strategy, much is still unknown about the process and effectiveness of collaborative arrangements such as CoC networks. We, therefore, use the context of homeless policy to study public-nonprofit collaborations and the ways that they are designed, lead and managed, and successful in achieving some level of effectiveness. Through this research, we have learned important lessons.

First, while communities and their incidence of homelessness vary, there are commonalities in how they are structured and governed. A majority of networks comprise multi-sector actors including schools, faith-based organizations, health and human service entities, government agencies, and nonprofit providers—just as the federal policy expected, diversity of stakeholder groups. In addition, networks tend to be led by nonprofit agencies and in some cases by government entities. Common governance arrangements include: shared leadership, lead agency, and network administrative organization (NAO).

Second, leadership is key and exhibited by Collaborative Applicants. Collaborative Applicants, as the designated agency responsible for submitting a single grant application to HUD and for managing federal resources on behalf of CoC networks, do play a critical role and utilize leadership style. Specifically, transformational leadership and collaborative leadership are used by Collaborative Applicants to lead and inspire members to work cohesively. Transformational leadership is used to build and manage relationships and collaborative leadership is useful for task-oriented behaviors such as network initiation, motivating members, and new member invitations. Our survey research and case study research suggest that leadership matters and is linked to effective network performance in terms of perceived performance and reported outcomes.

Third, the work of CoC networks is complex and multidimensional, with attempts to address the varied needs of people experiencing homelessness. In our work, we specifically study the healthcare efforts of CoC networks as individuals experiencing homelessness are less likely to access healthcare systems. Thus, we were interested in learning the degree to which networks were making an impact in this area of important work and health equity. We learned through our national survey work that

Table 7.1   Challenges reported by homeless network members (N = 79)

Challenge	Total	Percent[a] (%)
Health safety of staff	44	57
Reduction or loss of financial resources	39	51
Increased demand for services	33	43
Maintaining morale and motivation among our staff	31	40
Reduction or loss of available volunteers	28	36
Telecommuting is not appropriate for our line of work	26	34
Clients refusing to adhere to social distancing	25	33
Lack of personal protective equipment for our staff	22	29
Clients refusing to wear personal protective equipment	21	27
Other challenges	14	18
Unclear instructions from government agencies	13	17
Spread of COVID-19 among staff members	9	12
Lack of collaboration within the SLVCEH	3	4

[a]Percent value reflects the approximate percent of organizations out of total respondents that report that specific challenge
(*Source* Valero [2020])[1]

networks do engage in a large volume and variety of healthcare services from hosting clinics to street outreach to case management to substance abuse services and mental health treatment. Additionally, their success in this area is conditioned on capacity and resources at the community level.

Lastly, we can measure CoC network performance in multilevel ways including organizational, network, and community levels, and in our book, we identify ways that networks can assess and measure themselves. From this, we hope that CoC networks can explore the variety of ways that they can measure their performance and think critically about the factors that matter in explaining variation. We also review the key variables associated with network performance, including nonprofit leadership, network leading experience, network membership and leadership style.

The COVID-19 pandemic, however, generated significant challenges for CoC networks and put their strategies, experience, and passion for public service to the test. A survey of a CoC network in a Western state and specifically 79 homeless serving organizations found that they encountered challenges ranging from a lack of collaboration to reduction of financial resources (Valero 2020) (see Table 7.1).

Valero (2020) reported that CoC networks tend to exhibit resiliency by adopting innovative strategies focused on improving management and operations as well as the experiences of clients and staff (both paid and volunteer staff). Management strategies included participating in county-wide collaborative meetings, applying for federal funding, creating an internal response team, and building on existing partnerships. Client and staff strategies included working remotely, implementing health safety protocols, and surveying the needs of both staff and clients. Much remains to be understood about the degree to which CoC networks have fully recovered from the effects of the pandemic and the factors associated with effective performance during trying times.

Our book makes meaningful contributions to both theory and practice. From a theoretical perspective, we explore theories and areas of work, including the role of nonprofits and leadership in explaining CoC network effectiveness. Research on network performance and effectiveness is rare and that's largely because of the complexity and challenges surrounding measuring network outcomes. However, our work identified a framework by which to assess performance and the key theoretical pieces that matter. Our work also adds to the literature on collaboration with particular attention to homeless services, a fruitful yet understudied policy environment that is receiving much federal and state policy attention.

From a practitioner perspective, our research identified a number of strategies, methods, management skills, and more that people managing networks can utilize in their community-based work. We, for example, identify best practices of healthcare services that CoC networks tend to provide to their community. For networks looking to build their health-care capacity, our findings suggest specific programs that can be identified and implemented. Additionally, our work identifies the key leadership styles and behaviors that matter in leading collaborative networks. Our transformational leadership tool, for example, can be used by network managers to self-assess and identify areas of improvement and to consider ways of utilizing the leadership style in their own work. Lastly, networks

---

[1] Valero, N. J. 2020. Keeping open the doors of hope. How the coronavirus pandemic is affecting homeless services in Salt Lake County. Salt Lake City. Utah Foundation. Also available at https://www.utahfoundation.org/wp-content/uploads/rr777.pdf (Retrieved 9.2.2022).

are fluid entities that grow in different directions. We identify governance arrangements from our survey and case study work, which networks can use to assess their current and future governance arrangements. Networks, for example, can grow to the point of establishing their own self-standing nonprofit that is responsible for managing the affairs of the network.

Appendix 1: Leadership in Collaboration Survey

Section 1: Continuum of Care

The following set of questions are focused on understanding the composition of your Continuum of Care (CoC). Please answer each question carefully.

For how long has your CoC been in existence in your area?

- ○ Less than one year (1)
- ○ One year (2)
- ○ Two years (3)
- ○ Three years (4)
- ○ Four years (5)
- ○ Five years (6)
- ○ Other (please specify) (7) _____

For how long has your organization served as the lead agency (or Collaborative Applicant) for the CoC?

- ○ Less than one year (1)
- ○ One year (2)
- ○ Two years (3)
- ○ Three years (4)

H. S. Jang and J. N. Valero, *Public-Nonprofit Collaboration and Policy in Homeless Services*, https://doi.org/10.1007/978-3-031-11918-7

○ Four years (5)
○ Five years (6)
○ More than five years (7)

Approximately how many organizations are members of your CoC?
Does your CoC have membership meetings?

○ Yes (1)
○ No (2)

How often does your CoC membership meet?

○ About once a week (1)
○ About once a month (2)
○ About once every quarter (3)
○ About once a year (4)
○ Other (please specify) (5) _____

What percentage of the CoC membership attends meetings?

○ Less than 10% of membership (1)
○ 10–20% of membership (2)
○ 20–30% of membership (3)
○ 30–40% of membership (4)
○ 40–50% of membership (5)
○ 50–60% of membership (6)
○ 60–70% of membership (7)
○ 70–80% of membership (8)
○ 80–90% of membership (9)
○ 90–100% of membership (10)

Does your CoC use any of the following forms of communication to
maintain CoC members informed?

	Yes (1)	No (2)
E-mail (1)	○	○
Telephone (2)	○	○

(continued)

(continued)

	Yes (1)	No (2)
Written memo (3)	○	○
Membership meeting (4)	○	○
Social media (e.g., Facebook, Twitter) (5)	○	○
Individual visit to member organization (6)	○	○
Website (7)	○	○
Other (please specify): (8)	○	○

What are the key purposes of CoC collaboration? *Please identify the degree to which each of the following is a purpose of collaboration.

	Not a purpose (1)	Minor purpose (2)	Major purpose (3)
Access and share information (1)	○	○	○
Access and share resources (2)	○	○	○
Service enhancement (3)	○	○	○
Achieve economy of scale (4)	○	○	○
Shared accountability (5)	○	○	○
Linked to other CoC members (6)	○	○	○
End homelessness (7)	○	○	○

What are some challenges that your CoC has experienced in working together? *Please identify degree to which each of the following is a challenge for your CoC.

	No challenge (1)	Minor challenge (2)	Major challenge (3)
Power imbalance among member organizations (1)	○	○	○
Lack of capacity to work collaboratively (2)	○	○	○

(continued)

(continued)

	No challenge (1)	Minor challenge (2)	Major challenge (3)
Lack of effective communication (3)	○	○	○
Lack of accountability (4)	○	○	○
Lack of network sustainability (5)	○	○	○

If the CoC Collaborative Applicant agency had revenues during the most recently completed fiscal year, what percentage of your revenues came from the following sources?

_____ Government or public agencies (i.e., grants, fees): (1)
_____ Private donations: (2)
_____ Special events: (3)
_____ Dues / membership fees from member organizations: (4)
_____ Private sale of goods and services: (5)
_____ Other income (i.e., endowment, interest): (6)

How would you describe the governance of your CoC? <div> *Please select best answer. </div>

○ Shared Governance: the CoC is managed by all member organizations (1)
○ Lead Organization: a member organization of the CoC takes the lead (2)
○ Network Administrative Organization: CoC is managed by an administrative entity that is not involved in service provision (3)
○ Other (please specify) (4) _____

Is your CoC established as a 501(c)(3) public charity?

○ Yes (1)
○ No (2)

Section 2: Collaboration Outcome

The following set of questions are focused on understanding the degree to which your CoC is able to achieve collaboration outcomes. Please answer all questions.

In the last five years, to what extent has your CoC been able to achieve success in the following areas?

	(1) Did not experience success at all (1)	2 (2)	3 (3)	4 (4)	(5) Experienced success to a very great extent (5)	Did not make effort in this area (6)
Increase CoC membership (1)	○	○	○	○	○	○
Increase range of services (2)	○	○	○	○	○	○
Reduce the duplication of services (3)	○	○	○	○	○	○
Increase member commitment (4)	○	○	○	○	○	○

In the last five years, to what extent has your CoC been able to contribute value to the community it serves?

	(1) Did not experience success at all (1)	2 (2)	3 (3)	4 (4)	(5) Experienced success to a very great extent (5)	Did not make effort in this area (6)
Built greater awareness about homelessness (1)	○	○	○	○	○	○

(continued)

(continued)

	(1) Did not experience success at all (1)	2 (2)	3 (3)	4 (4)	(5) Experienced success to a very great extent (5)	Did not make effort in this area (6)
Decreased homelessness in the community (2)	○	○	○	○	○	○
Service cost lowered (3)	○	○	○	○	○	○

SECTION 3: STYLE OF LEADERSHIP

The following questions ask you to describe your style of leadership as you perceive it. Please answer all questions. How often do you engage in the following behaviors?

	(1) Never (1)	2 (2)	3 (3)	4 (4)	(5) Very Often (5)
Treating all network members as equals (1)	○	○	○	○	○
Identifying resources (2)	○	○	○	○	○
Identifying stakeholders (3)	○	○	○	○	○
Putting suggestions made by the network into operation (4)	○	○	○	○	○
Sharing leadership role with other network members (5)	○	○	○	○	○
Making sure individual roles are understood by the network members (6)	○	○	○	○	○
Asking that network members follow standard rules and regulations (7)	○	○	○	○	○
Selecting performance measures (8)	○	○	○	○	○

(continued)

(continued)

	(1) Never (1)	2 (2)	3 (3)	4 (4)	(5) Very Often (5)
Encouraging support from external stakeholders (9)	O	O	O	O	O
Establishing member commitment to the network's mission (10)	O	O	O	O	O
Publicizing the network's goals and accomplishments (11)	O	O	O	O	O
Using incentives to motivate network members (12)	O	O	O	O	O
Freely sharing information among network members (13)	O	O	O	O	O
Creating trust among network members (14)	O	O	O	O	O
Keeping work moving at a rapid pace (15)	O	O	O	O	O
Settling conflicts when they occur in the network (16)	O	O	O	O	O
Focusing efforts in building future leadership of network (17)	O	O	O	O	O
Expressing the need to adhere to ethical standards among members of the network (18)	O	O	O	O	O
Instilling fairness in the process of managing resources in the network (19)	O	O	O	O	O
Considering the needs of network members before those of my own organization (20)	O	O	O	O	O
Making an effort to build a network vision to internal and external stakeholders of the network (21)	O	O	O	O	O
Helping each member of the network understand their unique role in network mission (22)	O	O	O	O	O

(continued)

(continued)

	(1) Never (1)	2 (2)	3 (3)	4 (4)	(5) Very Often (5)
Inspiring network members to work cohesively for common purpose (23)	○	○	○	○	○
Expressing confidence in network members' ability to achieve network vision (24)	○	○	○	○	○
Being open to the ideas and suggestions of network members (25)	○	○	○	○	○
Seeking the counsel of key stakeholders of the network (26)	○	○	○	○	○
Helping network members look at issues from different perspectives (27)	○	○	○	○	○
Creating opportunities for network members to engage in creativity and innovation (28)	○	○	○	○	○
Paying special attention to the individual needs and challenges of network members (29)	○	○	○	○	○
Providing assistance to network members so that they are able to overcome challenges they encounter (30)	○	○	○	○	○
Helping assimilate new network members (31)	○	○	○	○	○
Teaching and coaching network members (32)	○	○	○	○	○

SECTION 4: THIS FINAL SECTION IS FOCUSED ON LEARNING MORE ABOUT YOU

What is your gender?

○ Male (1)
○ Female (2)

What is your race/ethnicity?

○ White (non-Hispanic) (1)
○ Hispanic/Latino (2)
○ Black or African American (3)
○ Asian (4)
○ Other: (5) _____

What is your age?

○ 21–30 (1)
○ 31–40 (2)
○ 41–50 (3)
○ 51–60 (4)
○ Over 61 (5)

What is your level of education?

○ Less than high school (1)
○ High school diploma or equivalent (2)
○ Some college (3)
○ Bachelor's degree (4)
○ Master, doctoral, or professional degree (5)

How long have you been working in the field of social services?

○ Less than one year (1)
○ From 1 to 5 years (2)
○ From 6 to 10 years (3)
○ From 11 to 20 years (4)
○ More than 20 years (5)

In what sector are you currently employed?

○ Public, government (1)
○ Public, school district (2)
○ Public, nonprofit hybrid organization (3)
○ Nonprofit (4)

○ Private (5)
○ Congregation (6)
○ Other (please specify) (7) _____

For how long have you been the contact person for the Collaborative Applicant or in a leadership position within the CoC?

○ Less than 1 year (1)
○ 1 year (2)
○ 2 years (3)
○ 3 years (4)
○ 4 years (5)
○ 5 years (7)
○ Other: (6) _____

Have you participated in any leadership training program in the past?

○ Yes (1)
○ No (2)

INDEX

© The Editor(s) (if applicable) and The Author(s), under exclusive
license to Springer Nature Switzerland AG 2023
H. S. Jang and J. N. Valero, *Public-Nonprofit Collaboration
and Policy in Homeless Services*,
https://doi.org/10.1007/978-3-031-11918-7

Preventive services, 52
Public housing agencies, 7

R
Racial inequality, 6
Reduced organizational autonomy, 61
Resource sharing, 61

S
School districts, 7
Service Network Administrative
    Organization (SNAO), 30
Shared governance, 28–30
Shared leadership, 34
Style of leadership, 33
Suboxone clinic, 53
Substance use, 46, 47
Supportive housing, 52, 53
Systemic barriers, 46

T
Task-oriented behaviors, 26

Transaction cost, 20
Transformational leadership, 34
2020 Annual Homeless Assessment
    Report, 3

U
Unaccompanied youth, 2
Unsheltered homeless, 3
Unsheltered homelessness, 5
Unsheltered youth, 3, 5
U.S. Department of Education, 2
U.S. Department of Housing and
    Urban Development (HUD), 2
U.S. Interagency Council on
    Homelessness (USICH), 9, 10

V
Volunteers, 18

W
Wicked problems, 14
Wrap-around case management, 52